MW00883595

Coming to America - The Francom Story

Editors Note: This is a rewriting of the Story found in the Journals of William and Amy Francom and William H. Francom and Joseph Francom and of Samuel Francom . This story has been romanticized to make for a fun read. Yet remaining true to the essence of Samuel and William's stories. The Editing was done by Martin Francom and rewriting assisted using "Open-AI" William and Amy are my Great, Great Grand Parents. As far as I know all the Francom's in America are descendants of William and Amy. My Francom Line goes → William & Amy Francom → William Henry Francom → Emeron Archibald Francom → Joseph Eugene Francom → Martin Eugene Francom (me).

Table Of Content:

From William and Amy's Journals:

In the annals of this tale, as far as our knowledge stretches, we find ourselves transported back to the year of our Lord 1815, when a child named William Francom made his entrance into this world. It is said that he was the illegitimate offspring of Elizabeth Francom, a woman of unknown origins. Some diligent soul has endeavored to uncover the faint traces of our ancestral line, harking back to a marriage twixt a certain Joseph Francom and a Guano Abbot in the year 1743, within the confines of Somerset, England. The fruit of their union, a son christened Joseph, came into being the following year, 1744 to be precise. This young Joseph entered into wedlock with a fair maiden named Mary Olds in 1765, and thus commenced a new chapter in our lineage. The third

Joseph in the lineage, born in 1765, emerged as a result of this sacred union. In due course, a fourth Joseph, progeny of this coupling, exchanged vows with a certain Mary Evans in 1788. These individuals, my good reader, were the ancestors of Elizabeth Francom, who bore the aforementioned William, whose paternal progenitor remains an enigma. In honor of his mother's maiden name, William proudly carried the Francom moniker. His affiliation with the Mormon Church, I dare say, has played a significant role in bringing us to this present moment. In the year 1837, he entered into holy matrimony with a lady by the name of Amy Harding.

Nine years after the nuptial bonds were forged between William and Amy, they embarked on a daring journey, accompanied by their three offspring, William Henry being the eldest son, George and Joseph to the distant lands of South Africa. A movement of colonization had taken hold, drawing adventurers to seek fortune and destiny in that direction. The motivations that spurred the Francom family to join this great migration have been lost to the tides of time. Some conjecture that it was William's father who, in his benevolence, provided the means to finance this expedition and set his son on a path to a new life. And so it was, dear reader, that they settled in a place called Uitenhage, a stone's throw away from the bustling Port Elizabeth in the Cape Colony.

Gather 'round, kin and kindred, and let me carry you on the breeze of time, back to days when life flowed as steady as the river's current and dreams were sewn like seeds in fertile soil.

Once William and Amy Francom set foot in the heart of Uitenhage, William Sr. decided to hitch his wagon to the winds of opportunity. With his son William Henry by his side, they conjured up a traveling emporium, a store that roamed the land on wheels, a sight as marvelous as a shooting star in a midnight sky. And let me tell you, William Sr. wasn't just a storekeeper, no siree, he had the touch of a blacksmith too, a man who could shape metal as easily as the wind shapes the dunes.

Now, imagine this, their emporium was no ordinary stall. Nay, it was a wagon of their own design, a portable haven of goods that held everything a body might desire. Oh, they peddled their wares, those useful treasures, to the Dutch farmers who tilled the earth like a mother tending to her children. And those farmers, they'd welcome that emporium like an old friend, with open arms and eager hearts.

But the story doesn't end there, oh no, for the tale is woven with threads of family and the strength of unity. Joseph, the third son, he had a tongue as silver as a moonbeam on water. He knew the Dutch tongue, you see, and he could dance with words like a minstrel with his strings. And so, he took the reins of the mobile store, driving it to the very doorsteps of Dutch homesteads, a modern marvel in those days.

As time waltzed on, William Sr. and his boys, they didn't just settle for peddling treasures on wheels. No sir, they cast their net wider, like fishermen reaching for the horizon. They built a blacksmith's haven, a place where fire danced with metal and the clang of hammers was music to their ears. And there, right next to it, they put up a watering hole, a place where stories were swapped as freely as the wind carries whispers.

And that wasn't the end of their tale, for they raised a brood, a hearty bunch of seven, a family that grew as naturally as a field of sunflowers. William and Amy, they were blessed with sons named William Jr., George, Joseph, John, Samuel, James and a daughters named Mary Ann.

So there you have it, a tale of enterprise and family, woven together like a quilt made of patches of sunsets and starlit nights. A tale where a father and his sons roamed the land with their emporium, a beacon of commerce in a world just beginning to stir, where a blacksmith's hammer was as important as a farmer's plow, and where dreams were etched in the sky like constellations waiting to be discovered.

From Samuel Francom's Memoirs:

In the year 1852, on the second day of January, I, Samuel Francom had the honor of entering this world in the quaint town of Uitenhage, situated in the Cape Colony of South Africa. I was the eighth offspring in a bustling brood of ten children, born to my English parents who had ventured to Africa in 1847. My father, William Francom, hailed from Bristol, England, his birth occurring on the fourth day of December in the year 1815.

Likewise, my mother, Amy Harding, was born on the twenty-fifth day of August in the year 1811, in Marla, England. Before our migration to Africa, my parents had already bid farewell to three of their children who had passed away in their homeland. The founding of Uitenhage traces its roots back to 1804 when DeMist, a notable figure, established this town on the banks of the Zwartkops river, approximately twenty miles away from Port Elizabeth. Recently, I received news that the streets of Uitenhage, adorned with

trees, now bear water channels, while two grand wool-washing establishments grace the river banks.   (Picture: Uitenhage Town Hall)

Port Elizabeth, it's a name that rings like a song, a song that's been echoing for centuries. Back in them days, when the land was raw and wild, that very port was just a tender sapling in the vast forest of Algoa Bay, to the east of Cape Recife. And you know who laid eyes on this gem first? A man named Bartholomew Diaz, he was the one who, in the year 1488, discovered this bay, like a treasure hidden in the earth's embrace.

But it wasn't until years later, like a tale that takes its time weaving its plot, that this land found itself cradled in the arms of settlers. Dutch settlements, like pioneers in a brave new world, stretched their fingers eastward in 1754, and oh, how Port Elizabeth found itself in their embrace. Those were times when the land was claimed not just by compass and map, but by the hearts of those who believed in the promise of a new dawn.

And then, oh, then came Colonel Vandeleur, a man with a vision etched like a roadmap in his mind. In 1799, he planted a flag in the earth, claiming his stake, and atop the Hill, just west of the Bookens River, a small fort rose, sturdy as a father's promise.

By the time 1820 came a-knockin', just a blink of an eye before my own folks would venture into this tale, Port Elizabeth, it was a place that hummed with life, like the heartbeats of a family gathered 'round a fire. But mind you, back then, it wasn't like the bustling metropolis you see today, no sir. The population, well, it was like a handful of stars in a vast night sky, a mere 35 souls to call it home, not counting the soldiers stationed to guard this little corner of the world.

But oh, don't let the numbers fool you, for it's in the whispers of those souls, it's in the footsteps of those soldiers, and it's in the very soil beneath our feet that the story of Port Elizabeth takes root. It's a tale that's been penned by hands weathered by time, a tale of discovery, of settlement, and of growth.

So there you have it, a piece of history wrapped in the folds of a folk tale, a tale of a port that started small but dreamed big, a tale that's still being written with every wave that kisses the shore and every heartbeat that calls this place home.

During my early years, my father toiled as a skilled blacksmith, employing his trade with diligence. I recollect, as a wee lad, he would perch me upon a sturdy box, guiding my little hands to fan the bellows. Oh, what a thrill coursed through my veins upon hearing the roar and witnessing the fiery blaze. However, around the year 1856, my father embarked upon a new endeavor—an enterprise in the realm of merchandise. Prior to this venture, our family had found residence in a row of modest three-room cottages. Yet, the burgeoning success of his trade prompted us to relocate to a splendid abode—a six-

room brick house crowned with a slate roof. The kitchen, a single elongated chamber, housed the fireplace, or as it was commonly referred to, the brick stove. All culinary endeavors were accomplished over an open fire or within the confines of that very brick oven. It is with fondness that I recall the delectable creations my mother would conjure—plump plum puddings, succulent roasts, and a medley of vegetables that danced upon the palate, unrivaled in flavor.

Gracing our surroundings were approximately two acres of fertile garden, its perimeter hugged by hedges adorned with white and yellow quince on one side, while pomegranate bushes flourished on the other. In addition to this botanical delight, an orchard thrived, boasting figs of varying hues—blue, white, and yellow—alongside clusters of grapes, pears, and apples. These bountiful fruits and vegetables, together with a cornucopia of produce, yielded a harvest thrice a year, thanks to the irrigation system nourished by the water flowing through ditches along the streets. This precious liquid emanated from a reservoir nestled within the hills overlooking the city.

Adjacent to our residence, our mercantile establishment stood proudly. Painted upon the store's facade was the sign that read, "Francom Mercantile & Grocery—Home of the Prince of Wales Feathers," accompanied by a charming depiction of said feathers. One of the grandest occasions of my youth in Africa manifested itself in the visit of the Prince of Wales, who would later ascend the throne as King George V of England. In honor of his presence, all the schoolchildren flocked to witness our Prince and pay homage. As he passed our humble abode, our hearts swelled with pride as he acknowledged our sign by pointing at it.

Opposite our store, a bustling market square unfolded its vibrant tableau. It served as a gathering place for gardeners, farmers, merchants, housewives, and anyone seeking to acquire goods. Here, a cornucopia of nature's bounty was put up for auction—fruits, vegetables, cheese, butter, and eggs—all traded with fervor. Horses and goats, too, found themselves in the spotlight, as prospective buyers vied for their possession. Goats were especially common, for they bestowed upon us the gift of milk. Moreover, this very square served as a stage for the dispensation of justice. Minor transgressions met their

reckoning through the whip, while more heinous crimes found their culprits swinging from the gallows at the center of the square. I, too, bore witness to these public hangings, as well as the disciplinary lashings.

My father's business with help from his son's William and George continued to thrive, expanding beyond the realm of dry goods and groceries to encompass wholesale meats and spirits, thereby fortifying his prosperity.

Even as a child, I possessed an unyielding energy that impelled me to aid my father by undertaking various errands. Our goods were procured from Port Elizabeth, and to transport this merchandise to Uitenhage, oxen-drawn wagons served as our sole means of transportation, as the land had yet to witness the advent of railroads. I have since come to learn, from reliable sources, that the Uitenhage of today, in the years spanning from 1920 to 1940, thrives primarily on the industry of railway workshops.
Now dear reader, let me spin you a tale from the annals of my yester-years, where family, the land, and the creatures of the wild danced together like fireflies on a summer's eve.

Now, my mother's sister, known by all as Aunt Tabby Croucher, lived a piece away, 'bout five miles or so from the heart of Uitenhage. Her man, a man with a touch of magic in his veins, he was a trapper and a hunter, a master of the wild. He'd ship off lions and tigers to England, creatures that roamed our lands like legends sprung to life. And he, with the help of two or three good-hearted Negro souls, ran a farm that thrummed with life, where the earth yielded its treasures and the sky painted its canvas.

Now, let's not dwell on the cruelty that can take root in any heart, for those days held their share of shadows. Those Negro laborers, they worked with hands that knew the soil's secrets, tended the land and the livestock, all for a sum that barely measured up to a dollar or a dollar and a half in a year's time. But they were clothed, they were fed, and they were part of a way of life that was common as the sun rising each morn. In those days, it was the way of things, not a reflection of the goodness in a man's heart.

But let's journey on to brighter memories, shall we? Many a time, I'd lace up my shoes of adventure and head on over to my aunt and uncle's abode. I can still hear his voice, my uncle's, ringing in the air like a songbird's melody. "Sammy," he'd call, "let's go gather some honey." And off we'd trot, like a pair of horses with the wind at their backs. You see, there's a bird, a bird with a heart full of collaboration, they call it the "Honey-Guide." It'd flit and flutter overhead, its tune a whistle that only our hearts could understand. With a trust in that feathered guide, we'd find the treasure of the bees, hidden away like secrets in the hills or the heart of rocky crevices. And there, with their boisterous chatters and their joyful twirls, those Honey Guides, they'd tell us where the gold of honey lay. And the menfolk, they'd gather barrels of the sweet stuff, enough to make your mouth water at the very thought.

Now, let's switch the scene to brighter days, where the play of children met the play of creatures. You see, we had our youthful antics, and some, they may have caused a critter a bit of discomfort. Those turtles, slow and steady, we'd pull 'em from the water, not for the sake of harm, but for the sake of a curious spirit. We'd flop them on their back, watching as they'd struggle to right themselves. But mind you, it wasn't cruelty that guided our hands, it was the fire of youthful curiosity. Eventually, we would loose interest and allow the turtles to wonder back to the pond from which they were plucked.

And then there were those giant tortoises, strong as the very hills they roamed. We'd clamber onto their shells like knights on horses, and there we'd go, riding 'round the land, slow and steady, like a river finding its way to the sea.

So there you have it, my friends, a piece of my past, where family, the land, and the creatures of the wild joined in a dance that spun the tapestry of my youth. Let's remember, every story's got its shades, but every shade holds a lesson, a lesson that's as bright as the sun that warms our days.

Sit yourselves down, dear listeners, and let me take you on a ride through the heart of adventures that'll raise your eyebrows and make your hearts race, just like a pack of horses set loose on a wild prairie.

Now, my uncle, he was a man who knew how to coax the land to give its best. His fields stretched out like a green sea, adorned with the bountiful treasures of squash and melons. But listen close, for it's not just the fruits of the earth that made our hearts race, it's the tricks we played in those fields that bring a glint to my eye even now.

Imagine, if you will, a mischievous band of young'uns, with more energy than a lightning bolt. We had this little game, a cunning game, you might say. We'd pierce tiny holes into those squash, just enough for a monkey's curious hand to slip inside. Oh, those monkeys, they'd come around, drawn by the scent of the seeds within. They'd plunge their hands in, thinking they've hit the jackpot. But oh, the tricky part is this – their little fists, once clamped around those seeds, would refuse to let go. And there they were, stuck like a mouse in a trap, and all we had to do was saunter over and scoop them up.

Now, one day, my brother William, he had luck on his side. He stumbled upon a wee baby monkey, innocent as a daisy in the morning dew. He handed it to me, with a chuckle that could rival the trickling brook. "Look," he said, "a baby Negro!" Now mind you, he was jesting, for this little creature had a hairless face, and in its smallness, it did bear a resemblance to a dark-skinned child. And when it let out its cries, oh dear, they sounded like the plaintive wails of a babe in need.

But don't let your minds linger too long in the fields, for we're taking a turn deeper into the heart of the land, where wild goats danced like the wind. One day, my dear brother William, the very same mischief-maker, and I set out to check his traps. Those traps, oh, they were baited with fresh meat, the kind that would tempt even the fiercest of creatures. Tigers and lions, they were our secret hope, but the traps remained untouched.

And as the day gave a gentle nod to dusk, the air around us came alive with a symphony of sounds – baboons chattering like a town full of gossiping women, monkeys adding their own tune to the melody, and the eerie, hair-raising screams of hyenas piercing through the canvas of the night. And there, in the distance, the king of the jungle himself, the lion, he roared his presence, a reminder that we were just guests in his domain.

Now, my brother William Henry, bless his mischievous heart, knew just how to yank my chain. He'd vanish into the jungle's embrace, like a ghost melting into the mist, leaving me with a heart that thudded like a drum. But fear not, for he'd come back, grinning like a cat who's caught a canary, his laughter like music to my ears, soothing the wild anxieties that danced in the corners of my mind.

So there you have it, a snippet from the pages of my youth, a tale woven with mischief, the thrill of the wild, and the bond between brothers that's as unbreakable as the spirit of the land itself.

Gather 'round, young and old, for I'm about to take you on a journey into the heart of the past, where oxen were the engines of progress and tales were spun with every step they took. You see, my father, a man as practical as a plow, had a knack for getting things done. And to help him harness the power of those brawny oxen, he hired two African men whose strength rivaled that of a mountain storm. With those strong arms guiding the way, we had five teams of oxen, each yoked up and ready for action. And what a sight that was, friends! Five teams, led by men whose whips cracked like a summer thunderstorm, pulling a load that could make the earth itself bow down.

And so, many a dawn found us on the road, a procession of hooves and wheels forging through the untamed wilderness. Our destination? Port Elizabeth, a name that conjured images of distant shores and bustling harbors. A twenty-mile journey it was, a stretch that could make the sun sweat and the moon rise early.

But let me tell you, that path was no well-trodden road, no sir! It was a trail etched by the feet of those who dared venture where no human dwelling dared interrupt the vast expanse of nature. Trees stood tall like ancient sentinels, their branches whispering secrets to the wind. Rivers flowed like veins of the land, singing their own songs as they wound through the landscape.

And then, there it was, like a jewel in the rough, Port Elizabeth perched upon a hillside, overlooking the harbor. It was a place that hummed with the energy of progress, a hummingbird's heart in the chest of the land. And what caught the eye more than anything was the grand endeavor underway: a breakwater being constructed, a giant's puzzle made of massive rocks.

Teams of oxen, not so different from our own, hauled those colossal stones like ants on a mission. The ground shook beneath their steps, and their sweat mingled with the sea breeze. It was a scene of determination, a dance between man and beast, as they hauled those rocks to build a fortress against the raging waves.

And here's the kicker, my friends, seventy-five years later, the same tale echoes. That breakwater, that mammoth puzzle, is still under construction, in my mind. So, as I sit by the fire and write this tale, I remember the oxen, the African hands, and the harbor's ambitious endeavor. So dear reader, remember for in every journey, no matter how long it takes, there's a tale waiting to be lived and a story waiting to be told.

One summer's morn, with the sun still stretching and yawning, I found myself caught up in another memorable escapade. It was one of those journeys that dance in your memory like fireflies on a warm southern night. My father, a man as sturdy as an oak tree, decided it was high time to pay a visit to our kinfolk, cousins who dwelled a good spell away. And so, with the excitement of a barn dance and the practicality of a well-packed saddlebag, we embarked.

Now, to reach those kin, we had to cross two rivers that, let me tell you, were no less than titans. One of these mighty waters, it's etched into my recollection like a brand on a steer's hide, was the Gamtoos River. But before we got to that, our journey unfurled like a grand map of adventure. For two days and nights, we rode beneath the vast expanse of the open sky, our campfires dotting the landscape like stars fallen to the earth.

And oh, what nights those were! As we laid down to rest, the rocky cliffs above whispered secrets to the wind, while the distant roars of lions prowling in the ink-black night made our spines tingle. We were visitors in their wild kingdom, humble as a mouse in a hay barn.

Finally, our hooves carried us to the doorstep of our cousins' dwelling. But mind you, this wasn't your ordinary doorstep. No, sir! The skins of lions and tigers, creatures of myth and legend, adorned their floors. It was as if the beasts themselves had come to rest beneath our feet, leaving a mark of their untamed spirits.

And then, my friends, came the crossing of the Gamtoos River, a name that rolled off the tongue like a river's current. We stepped onto a ferry, a floating raft held together by the hopes of travelers and the sturdy hands of the ferryman. The river carried us, like a melody carries a songbird, to the other side. The land there was like a treasure trove of adventure waiting to be discovered.

So, onward we went, deeper into the heart of the land, riding atop horses as sturdy as the mountains, pulling a cart laden with our supplies. What was the purpose of this expedition, you ask? Well, that's the thing, my friends. Time has a way of muddling details like an autumn rain, washing away the specifics. But what I do remember, clear as the sound of a banjo at a hoedown, is that my father and I, side by side, faced the great unknown. Just the two of us, carving a path through the wild, like characters in a tale spun by the very fabric of the land itself.

One particular trip to Port Elizabeth with my brother, Joseph, remains etched in my memory. Before reaching the town, we camped on the outskirts of the jungle, sleeping on the bare ground beneath the open sky. The following morning, as Joe awakened me, he nonchalantly removed the blanket covering us. To my astonishment, coiled beside me lay a formidable poisonous snake, its girth comparable to that of a man's wrist, measuring five or six feet in length. Reacting swiftly, my brother seized my leg, pulling me away from the serpent, which uncoiled and slithered into the dense foliage. The danger had dissipated before I fully comprehended its presence.

The young lads of our town often flocked to the river for a refreshing swim. Located at a distance from town, it neighbored the "pest house" or hospital. During those times, a dreadful outbreak of black smallpox had gripped the community, leaving people in a state of alarm. Mandatory vaccination had been enforced by the government.

11

On a fateful day, as a group of us boys returned from our aquatic escapade, a hearse passed us, solemnly conveying patients who had succumbed to the smallpox epidemic. Spontaneously, we hopped on the rear of the hearse, stealthily entering its confines, and traveled into town, ensuring we disembarked before anyone caught sight of us. In retrospect, I can only envision the wrath my parents would have unleashed upon me had they ever discovered this audacious exploit!

Mormon Elders came to Uitenhage on my twelfth birthday preaching the gospel. At the time Mormonism was a most unpopular faith, but my parents, especially my mother, embraced its essence and claimed it resonated with their souls, aligning with their understanding of the sacred scriptures. Thus, they willingly embraced this newfound religion, marking a turning point in my own existence and that of my kin. The spirit of congregating in the Land of Zion descended upon us. Despite being aware of the persecution endured by the Church, which forced them from Kirkland, Missouri to Nauvoo, Illinois, and ultimately to the wild Utah Territory in the Rocky Mountains, we remained undeterred. nestled

In the year 1862, my eldest brother, William Henry along with Joseph, my third eldest sibling ventured to America. Then, in 1864, my father granted mother his consent to depart Africa with the children and embark on a journey to America. At that time, my father's business flourished to such an extent that my second eldest brother, George, had to remain in Africa to assist him in settling his affairs before eventually joining the rest of us in this new land.

From William Henry's and Joseph's Story:

In 1862, the brothers, William Henry and Joseph Francom embarked on an incredible journey from their home in Cape Town, South Africa to the vast and unknown lands of Utah Territory. They were devout Mormon converts, drawn to the promise of a new life and religious freedom in the American West. Little did they know that their journey

would be fraught with challenges and adventures beyond their wildest imagination.
As the brothers set sail from Cape Town, a ferocious storm descended upon their ship, testing their resolve and faith. The tempest raged for days, tossing the vessel like a mere toy in the hands of an angry sea. Joseph and William clung to the hope that they would survive, praying fervently for deliverance. Eventually, the storm subsided, leaving the brothers in awe of the immense power of nature and the fragility of human life.

Their voyage across the Atlantic was also marked by the haunting specter of the American Civil War. As they sailed closer to the United States, they encountered ships bearing the scars of battle, with wounded soldiers and stories of unimaginable atrocities. The brothers witnessed the devastating impact of the war, leaving an indelible mark on their hearts and minds.

Arriving in New York City, Joseph and William were captivated by its bustling streets and towering buildings. They marveled at the diversity of cultures and the vibrant energy that filled the air. And on every street corner it seemed there were recruiters for the Union Army. But Joseph with his ability to speak the Dutch Afrikaner language was able to assure them that we were Religious Pilgrims and would be as of no use as soldiers. So with their hearts longing for the promised land, they soon set off on a journey to Palmyra, a town in upstate New York that held great significance for their faith.

In Palmyra, the brothers retraced the steps of Joseph Smith, the founder of the Mormon faith, and experienced a profound connection to their religious heritage. They learned of the trials faced by early Mormon pioneers and drew strength from their resilience. Inspired by their predecessors' stories, Joseph and William continued their trek westward, venturing into the untamed frontier.

As they ventured westward, the land began to change, and the once familiar faces of settlers became scarce. It was during this time that they found themselves on the outskirts of Far West, Missouri, where their faith was met with both curiosity and skepticism. The locals eyed them with a mix of apprehension and intrigue, for the Mormons were still seen as outsiders in those parts.

One evening, as the sun dipped below the horizon, the brothers camped near a small stream, surrounded by the gentle rustling of prairie grass. Little did they know that this serene night would soon be interrupted by a band of Shawnee Indians who approached with curious eyes and cautious steps.

Fear gripped the brothers' hearts as they had only heard tales of Shawnee, and stories of clashes between the indigenous tribes and settlers had reached their ears. However, something in the Shawnee's demeanor made William and Joseph sense that they meant no harm.

With trepidation in their voices, they greeted the Shawnee, who responded with a traditional gesture of friendship. The brothers couldn't speak Shawnee language, and Shawnee couldn't understand English, yet the language of respect and goodwill bridged the gap between their cultures.

Shawnee offered them food, and the brothers gratefully accepted. As they sat around the campfire, sharing stories through gestures and expressions, William and Joseph felt an overwhelming sense of connection. They realized that beneath the surface, they were not so different after all.

For a few days that followed, the Shawnee tribe traveled alongside the brothers, guiding them through the vast and sometimes perilous terrain. They learned from each other – the brothers teaching the Shawnee about their faith and the Shawnee sharing their knowledge of the land and survival skills.

Through this journey, moments of fear were eclipsed by profound understanding. William and Joseph recognized the importance of respect and mutual cooperation in building a life in this new land. They realized that compassion and open-mindedness could overcome any divide between cultures.

Finally, the day came when they reached the outskirts of the Utah Territory. The Shawnee bid farewell to the brothers, who parted as friends, their hearts heavy with gratitude and the promise of enduring friendship.

As William and Joseph stood at the threshold of their new home, they carried with them not only the tenets of their faith but also the invaluable lesson of empathy. Their journey taught them that in the vast tapestry of humanity, differences are to be celebrated, not feared.

In the years that followed, the two brothers thrived in the embrace of their Mormon community, but they never forgot the Shawnee tribe that had shown them kindness on their path to Utah. They advocated for understanding and cooperation between settlers and indigenous peoples, becoming the catalyst for change in their new land.

Now, listen closely, and I'll take you down a winding trail of bravery and the kind of struggle that makes a person's spirit shine like a fire on a moonless night.

In the Southern Party of the Utah Territory where the earth stretched wide and the rivers ran wild, William and Joseph two souls that were embarking on a journey that would etch their names in the book of courage. You see, the Colorado River, it wasn't just any river. It was a giant, a force of nature that roared and rumbled like an angry bear.

Crossing it, well, that was a task that'd make a grown man's knees quake like leaves in the wind. The currents were swollen, frothing like a pot boiling over, and as they looked out at that river, Joseph and William knew they were facing a trial like none other. It was like staring into the eyes of a dragon guarding its treasure.

But let me tell you, these two young men weren't the kind to back down from a challenge, oh no. They had determination in their hearts, the kind of determination that could move mountains and part seas. With every step they took towards that river's edge, they were stepping into a battle, a battle against the very elements of nature.

Now, it wasn't just their courage that carried them through. Fate has a way of bringing kind-hearted souls into our paths, and that's exactly what happened. Locals, folks who knew the river's moods like a mother knows her child's laughter, lent their hands and hearts to these two brave souls. They guided them, whispered the river's secrets, and helped them find the threads of safety in that raging tapestry of water.

And so, hand in hand with determination and aided by the hands of kind locals, Joseph and William stood against that mighty river. They held tight to ropes, their fingers gripping like the roots of an oak tree, and they pushed against the current, each step forward a victory over fear. The river, it raged and roared, it tugged and pulled, but these two souls, they stood like titans, unyielding in the face of the storm.

The waters were treacherous, yes, but they weren't unbeatable. With every inch they conquered, with every heartbeat that matched the river's rhythm, Joseph and William moved closer to victory. The river's roars were matched with their own determined shouts, their spirits rising like the sun breaking through storm clouds.

And then, my friends, a moment came when they stood on the other side, the water dripping from their clothes like tears of triumph. The Colorado River, it had tested them, oh it had tested them good, but it hadn't broken them. They had faced its might, stared into its depths, and emerged as victors, two souls who'd braved the storm and lived to tell the tale.

So remember, as you sit by the fire and read this tale, that challenges may come like raging rivers, but with determination, with the helping hands of kind folks, the providence of God and with the strength that resides deep in the human heart, those challenges can be faced, those rivers can be crossed, and victory can be claimed, one step at a time.

Finally, after enduring a journey of countless trials and tribulations, the brothers arrived in Salt Lake City, the heartland of the Mormon faith. The sight of the construction of the magnificent Salt Lake Temple which would stand tall against the backdrop of the majestic Rocky Mountains brought tears of joy to their eyes. They had made it.

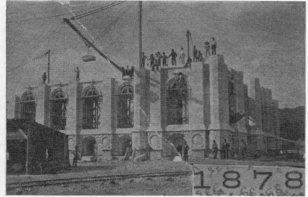

They hope to be able to help with the construction of the Temple but knew their destiny was in the hand of God. William and Joseph soon be separated. William being sent to help settle the Cashe Valley area north of what is know as the city of Logan. While Joseph was sent south to then Payson area, where he made preparations for the arrival of the rest of the family in 1865.

In the years that followed, Joseph and William would go on to play pivotal roles in the growth and development of their community. They worked tirelessly to build a prosperous settlements in various locations, nurturing the bonds of brotherhood and embodying the enduring spirit of the Mormon pioneers. They prepared for the soon arrival of the rest of their family.

Their incredible journey from Cape Town to Utah Territory stood as a testament to their unwavering faith, resilience, and the indomitable human spirit. The tales of Joseph and William became legendary, inspiring generations to come and reminding them that even in the face of the greatest adversities, there is always hope and the possibility of a better tomorrow. William in his later years would tell his Grand Children the most heart felt and meaningful stories fill with practical advise and wisdom. And so, the tale of William and Joseph echoes through time, reminding us that even in the face of uncertainty and differences, compassion and respect can weave the threads of harmony, creating a stronger and more united nation for generations to come.

Continuing From William and Amy's story:

On the first day of March in the year 1864, Brother Atwood and Brother Francom found themselves in a peculiar situation. They had decided to embark on a grand adventure with their families, journeying all the way from South Africa to the Utah Territory. The prospect of such a voyage was both thrilling and daunting, but these brothers in faith were determined to make it happen. Brother Francom, Amy's husband would be remaining behind with to finish up his business affairs.

Brother Atwood, being the more adventurous of the two, had a reputation for finding himself in humorous predicaments. Brother Francom, on the other hand, was the practical one, always armed with a solution for every problem. Together, they made quite the team, ready to conquer any challenge that came their way. They embarked upon the arduous task of organizing a band of South African colonists, new members of the Mormon Church for their migration to the United States, with the ultimate destination set for the distant lands of the untamed Utah Territory.

Their first task was securing supplies for the long journey. Brother Atwood, with his knack for exaggeration, insisted they needed enough food to feed a small army. "We mustn't forget the essentials," he declared, "such as barrels of pickles and crates of hot sauce! We can't possibly survive without them!"

Brother Francom, rolling his eyes, managed to convince Brother Atwood to scale back on the unnecessary condiments. They settled for more practical provisions like flour, dried meat, and beans. However, Brother Atwood snuck in a few jars of his favorite spicy relish, much to Brother Francom's dismay.

With supplies in tow, the brothers then set out to make arrangements for their passage. They visited the local port and met a rather peculiar ship captain named Captain Barnaby of the good ship Mexicana. Captain Barnaby was known for his unorthodox methods and quirky sense of humor. When the brothers inquired about the cost of passage, Captain Barnaby stroked his beard and said, "Well now, lads, I have a proposition for you. You see, my ship is not just any ship. It's a magical vessel!" Both Brother Atwood and Brother Francom exchanged skeptical glances. Magical ship? They had heard tales of Captain Barnaby's shenanigans, but this was something entirely different. Nevertheless, intrigued by the prospect, they asked him to explain further.

Captain Barnaby leaned in and whispered conspiratorially, "You see, my ship has a secret power. It can transform into a giant seagull and fly through the skies!"
Brother Atwood's eyes widened with excitement, while Brother Francom couldn't hide his skepticism. "Are you quite serious, Captain? A flying seagull ship?" he asked, trying to keep a straight face. Captain Barnaby burst into laughter, revealing that it was all just a joke. Passage , he said, would be 20 pounds, 25 if they wanted a private Cabin. The

ship, though not magical, was indeed seaworthy and could take them to their destination safely. Brother Atwood playfully punched Captain Barnaby's arm, saying, "You almost had me there, Captain! Imagine soaring through the skies on a winged ship!"

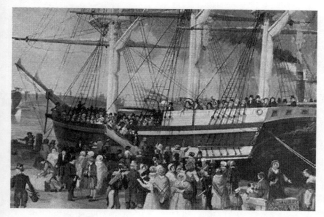

With their passage secured and their supplies stowed away, the group Mormon converts bid farewell to South Africa and set sail America. The journey was anything but smooth sailing, with stormy seas and mischievous dolphins splashing them with water just for fun. Brother Atwood, always finding humor in the most unlikely situations, laughed off the antics of the mischievous sea creatures, shouting, "Brothers, I think these dolphins mistook us for circus performers!"

Among the company, was the presence of Amy Francom and her children: John, Samuel, Mary Ann, and James. The father, William, spent the night aboard with them, bidding them farewell as the ship rested in the harbor. He chose to remain in South Africa with his son, George, while his sons William, Joseph, had already migrated to the Utah Territory several years previous.

Samuel's Story Continues:

The decision, let me tell you, wasn't a mere turn of the cards for my mother. No sir, it was like wrestling a grizzly bear between leaving behind her warm hearth, her good man, and her own flesh and blood sister. The poor woman must have had her soul churned up like a riverboat's paddle-wheel caught in a whirlpool. But, by the splendor of the stars, her faith stood taller than a Limpopo River steamboat's smokestack. It was like an anchor she tied around her heart, pulling her toward the Mormons, the very folks who sung a different hymn from the rest.

And as the days un-spooled like a lazy river, she showed the mettle of a true pioneer woman, hardy as a wildcat, plowing through the rocky fields of life. Those trials and

19

tribulations, well, they came thick as flies on a honey-drenched pie in July. But not once, let me tell you, not once did I catch wind of her muttering a word of bellyaching or waving a white flag of despair. She held on like a riverboat gambler holding a royal flush, all confidence and no bluster.

Now, why, you might ask, would anyone trade the comforts of their home for a leap into the great unknown? Well, it's a tale as knotty as a thicket of Southern backwoods. The Latter Day Saints, you see, were like a band of troubadours singing their gospel, but they had more troubles than a cat's got whiskers. They were pushed and prodded, like cattle headed to a new pasture, leaving behind scorched earth and angry folks.

And so, like a thief in the night, my dear mother slipped away. Hush-hush, like a raccoon sneaking into a chicken coop. Not a soul in the village knew she was bound for new horizons, except my old man. He held the secret close, tighter than a miser's grip on his gold.

One morning, when the birds were still rubbing the sleep from their eyes, my father loaded us onto those rickety wagons. Oxen were hitched up like a parade of grumbling giants, plowing through the morning mist. One Negro led the way, his steps falling like the beat of a forgotten melody, while another followed, his whip snapping like an impatient river.

As the sun yawned and stretched toward the horizon, we rolled into Port Elizabeth. Our belongings were shuffled onto that ship like a gambler's deck of cards in a high-stakes poker game. The inn we bedded down in was as plain as a barn dance on a Sunday morning. But the excitement inside was thicker than molasses, as we imagined the vast ocean awaiting us like an uncharted territory.

That night, sleep didn't come easy. It hung over us like a fog, thick and mysterious. The morrow held promises as vast as the prairie, and by every tick of the clock, we were one step closer to the grand adventure that awaited us on the open sea.

The ship accommodated 35 families, all devout followers of the Mormon Church, alongside the Captain and crew. Alongside the passengers, the vessel carried a cargo comprising hides, tallow, and wool, all bound for America. Most of the day was consumed by the loading process and settling in for the impending journey. Father accompanied us on board, and as the time to bid farewell drew near, a heavy melancholy hung in the air.

20

We were well aware that this parting might be our last, although his intentions were to follow us as soon as circumstances permitted. They were devout Mormon converts, drawn to the promise of a new life and religious freedom in the American West. Little did they know that their journey would be fraught with challenges and adventures beyond their wildest imagination.

During the night, our modest sailing vessel, the Brig Mexicanna, commenced its voyage. The next morning, as we arose and ascended to the deck, we caught sight of the distant shoreline. It was then that we congregated, hearts burdened to the brink of breaking. In unison, we raised our voices and sang:

"Oh, my native land, I hold thee dear,
Every scene I cherish, every memory clear,
Friends and kin, oh, joyous domain,
Can I bid thee farewell, bear the pain?

Can I leave thee? Can I leave thee?
To distant lands, my dwelling stray,
Can I, oh, can I say farewell?"

And so it came to pass that we settled into the rhythm of our lives aboard that vessel, with all things proceeding smoothly, except for the intermittent bouts of seasickness that afflicted us all. I recall being one of the last to succumb to its grip, finding great amusement in the misfortune of the younger ones. But alas, the cruel hand of fate turned upon me, and in my eyes, I suffered the most severe of all afflictions. Yet, in due course, we all recovered from our wretched seasickness and regained our strength as we neared the equator.

William & Amy Francom's Story Continued:

Time elapsed, and about six weeks passed since the preparations began until the day when the vessel set sail, carrying 42 members of the South African colony, 35 of whom were Mormons or potential Mormons, bound for New York. From there, we would undertake the arduous journey to fulfill our dreams in the promised land of the Utah Territory. It was on April 2, 1864, at noon, that the anchor was lifted, and the voyage began in earnest.

The daily account of our sea voyage presents a stark contrast to the present-day mode of travel. Yet, it was deemed a reasonably comfortable journey for its time. We were confined to two compartments, one for men and another for women and younger children. Brother Atwood, took it upon himself to establish a set of rules and regulations. One such rule stated that smoking was only permitted on the deck, strictly prohibited within the confines of the compartments. He diligently supervised the cleanliness of these quarters, no easy task considering it also served as storage for our belongings and food. With their own cook and steward, they utilized the ship's galley to prepare our meals. He warned his party against lodging complaints with the captain or accepting any form of medication or assistance from him.

In the long span of two months and four days, confined together as they were, it was inevitable for tensions to mount. There were squabbles and occasional rebellions against the established rules, with the women being particularly vocal in their grievances. Amy Francom, it must be noted, assumed the title of "chief of the grumblers" within our group.

Now, lean in close, and I'll spin a yarn for you, a tale that dances on the edge of mischief and the journey of souls across the vast sea.

Picture it, dear readers, the second day of our voyage, a ship cutting through the waves like a knife through butter. But you see, this ship wasn't just a vessel for adults, oh no. It carried the laughter and the spirit of young'uns too, a school of little fish swimming in the great ocean of life.

A school, you ask? Oh yes, a school right there on the ship's deck. Can you imagine? Bro. Atwood, a man as steady as the North Star, he stepped up as their teacher, along with two others who took their turns guiding these young minds. Now, let me tell you, the ship might've been rocking with the waves, but these souls, they were as eager as a mare let loose in a green pasture.

But ah, as every tale goes, there's a twist in the wind. There was this young sprout named Samuel Francom, a wild spirit if there ever was one. Unresponsive to reprimands, oh my, he was like a colt that refused to be tamed. And yes, there were times when the winds of authority had to be unfurled. Twice, if my memory serves right, they had to tie him to the ship's mast, like a bird whose wings needed a rest. There he'd stay, 'til his promise to behave was as solid as a promise given to the moon.

Now, hold on to your seats, for the tale doesn't end there. Samuel's brother, John, well, he decided to try his luck with a similar escapade. Aye, you guessed it, he met the same fate, tethered to the mast like a ship in harbor, until his promise to sail the seas of good behavior was sealed.

And there you have it, my friends, two young souls dancing on the precipice of mischief, leaving their mark on the pages of Bro. Atwood's journal. Oh, it's a peculiar pathway, this one, to the realm of immortality. For you see, even in their playful defiance, these boys carved their names in the story, forever etched as part of that ship's journey across the waves.

So remember, as you walk the pathways of life, that even the mischievous moments, the ones where spirits roam like wild horses, they too have a way of leaving their footprints in the sands of time. And sometimes, just sometimes, it's the incorrigible ones who find themselves remembered as the stars in a tale that spans generations.

Gather 'round, for I've got a tale that'll take you through the crests and troughs of a journey that sailed the waters of fate.

Now, picture this: each day dawned with the rising sun like a promise kept, and as the sun dipped below the horizon, we gathered like kin in prayer, morning and night, within the cozy nooks of our compartments. Guards stood sentinel through the silent watches of the night, their shadows dancing like stories told in the flicker of lantern light. Their watchful eyes, like guardian angels, ensured the cloak of safety wrapped around us as we dreamt.

But, oh my friends, even the mightiest ship ain't immune to mischief. Twice, the specter of "the devil" himself cast his shadow upon our decks. Whispers like ghostly winds, he tried to sow discord among the crew and the souls on board, like a trickster playing his hand. Yet, let me tell you, there's a power greater than the mischief of dark spirits, and that power, my friends, is prayer. With hearts woven in faith, we conjured a shield that sent that devil packing. His mischief, like smoke on a windy day, dissipated, and he achieved little in his malevolent endeavors.

But life at sea, it ain't all smooth sailing, oh no. Sickness, like a cloud that comes and goes, settled upon us like a shadow. And oh, how it pained our hearts when one among us, a dear soul with dreams woven in the threads of the sea breeze, succumbed. With heavy hearts and tear-filled eyes, we laid them to rest in the cradle of the vast ocean, their journey coming to an end, but their spirit forever carried on the wings of the wind.

Amidst the rhythm of the waves and the chorus of prayers, we caught glimpses of other ships, like fellow travelers on the same cosmic road. And oh, the sea, she's a generous host. We watched the graceful flight of fish, like dancers on the grand stage of the ocean, their shimmering scales reflecting the sun's embrace. And if luck was on our side, we'd bear witness to the grandeur of an occasional whale, a creature of myth and majesty, a true testament to the wonders of this watery realm.

But my friends, as much as we marveled at the sea's gifts, there came a torment that tested even the bravest of souls. Bedbugs, vile creatures, they invaded our cramped compartments like unwelcome guests. They nipped and gnawed, leaving trails of itch and discomfort. Yet, even in the face of this pesky plague, we bore it with a grin. For you see, these bedbugs, they were but a minor price to pay, a mere pinprick on the canvas of our dreams.

So remember, as you sail through life's waters, that even in the midst of challenges, even when the specters of discord and discomfort come knocking, there's a power in unity, in prayer, and in the shared dream of distant shores that can steer us through the darkest of storms and bring us safely to the sunrise of our dreams.

Finally, on the nineteenth day of June, the Mexicana arrived in the harbor of New York. Our stay in the bustling city lasted for a mere day. The following day, we embarked on a journey "by stagecoach" to Palmyra, and from there, our path led us to Far West where we were ferried across the mighty Mississippi. Our journey continued, taking us though Indian Territory. Fortunately with God's helping hand, our company crossed the Indian Territory without incidence and eventually, they arrived in the Utah Territory.

The Voyage from Samuel's Story:

"Sister Amy Francom and her children, John, Samuel, Mary Ann, and James," were baptized in the Colorado River. Then, on July 21, the arrival of 66 wagons, prepared to carry the Saints further west. At this point they meet up with other converts from England and continued their journey. The air hung heavy and oppressive, sweltering in its heat, and not a soul could escape its relentless grip. The ocean, in contrast, lay tranquil and serene, devoid of even the slightest ripple. So calm was its surface that we could peer down into its depths, observing the gentle sway of seaweed and the graceful dance of dolphins. And there, too, were the remarkable flying fish, emerging from the water and occasionally landing upon our deck. No breath of wind stirred our sails, leaving our ship adrift, its every canvas raised in futile display. In the dead of night, a feeble zephyr whispered its presence, growing in strength by morn. I overheard the Captain and his mates casting out the life buoy, seeking to measure our vessel's speed, which they declared to be a respectable ten knots per hour. They wore a look of contentment upon their faces, pleased with the progress we made. That very morning, as the watchman bellowed a warning, we learned of a whale crossing our path. The Captain commanded the ship to alter its course, allowing us to pass by the majestic creature. It spouted forth great fountains of water, resembling a mountain amid the vast expanse of the ocean. And so it was that we encountered several more whales and countless schools of flying fish on our maritime journey.

Days passed, and the first mate approached the Captain, sharing a foreboding premonition of an impending storm. The Captain raised his eyes to the heavens, offering some remark, before retiring to his cabin. In a short span, he emerged once more, issuing orders for the passengers to seek shelter below deck, while the men furiously worked to lower the sails. Even as the sailors scrambled up the masts to furl the final canvas, the tempest descended upon us with unbridled fury. Its savage might shattered one of the yardarms, hurling it and a hapless crewman to the deck. A fragment of the yardarm dangled precariously over the side, prompting the Captain's command to sever it, allowing it to drift away and cease its troublesome tug on the vessel's balance. Upon hearing the Captain's decree, I dashed towards a lifeboat and concealed myself beneath its shelter, driven by a morbid curiosity to witness the unfolding chaos. Oh, how I witnessed it all, but as the tempest raged on, I fervently wished I had heeded the Captain's instructions. During that fierce gale, I clung to ropes for dear life, desperate

to prevent the sea's insatiable hunger from claiming me. The Captain, lashed to the helm, fought with grim determination to steer our beleaguered ship. Once the storm had spent its wrath, he confided in his mate, revealing that we had been driven astray, a staggering 150 miles off our intended course. The hurricane had waged its assault for two long hours.

The following day, the crew diligently repaired the broken yardarm, unfurled the sails anew, and we resumed our journey with renewed swiftness. All souls on board reveled in the warm embrace of sunlight, grateful to have survived the drenching of the previous night. It was then that the watchman's voice pierced the air, urgently declaring, "Something looms ahead!" The Captain retrieved his spyglass, directing the helmsman to veer to the leeward. And there, before our eyes, lay a vessel, upturned and abandoned to the merciless sea. The Captain informed us that it was undoubtedly the wreckage of a ship that had succumbed to the storm the previous night. As it drifted past us, the watchman alerted us to another object adrift in the waves. The Captain issued orders to steer towards it, and upon investigation, it was revealed to be a fragment of the wrecked vessel's deck. The men towed it aboard our ship, destined to be carried to New York City as evidence of the tragedy. Barrels bobbed in the water, and amidst them, a solitary corpse, a grim reminder of the ocean's wrath.

Among our company, one of our brethren, Curshaw, fell ill, while a member of the ship's crew also lay in the throes of sickness. Both hovered precariously between life and death for a considerable time. Alas, our dear brother succumbed to his ailment and found his eternal rest within the embrace of the sea. With heavy hearts burdened by his memory, we sailed forth, often battling contrary winds, which impeded our progress.

After an arduous and wearisome journey, we finally reached the shores of New York. Merely three days away from the city's embrace, we encountered a tugboat sent to guide us into the harbor. The Captain arranged for our ship to be towed, a laborious process that spanned from the morning of Saturday until the evening of Sunday. That night, the Captain dropped anchor, and come daybreak, he ventured ashore, attending to the arrangements for cargo and passengers. The ensuing Monday was consumed by the procedures of the inspection office and customs house, where our belongings underwent meticulous scrutiny. Some among our group sought respite in a hotel that night, while others sought shelter within Castle Garden, which presently stands in the stead of Ellis Island.

It was at this precise moment, as the Civil War drew to a close, that we beheld soldiers, worn and battle-weary, returning to their homes. One vessel, in particular, caught our attention as it lay anchored in the harbor. The Marines aboard the ship regaled us with their band's harmonious strains each morning and night. After months spent at sea, their musical offerings brought solace and cheer to our weary souls.

Weary indeed we were, yearning for respite, yet Tuesday brought the call to board a train, commencing our westward journey. The train was crowded with soldiers making their way home, and at each station, poignant scenes unfolded as they disembarked to reunite with their loved ones. Laughter mingled with tears, for some rejoiced, while others mourned the sons they would never embrace again.

Upon our arrival in St. Louis, we embarked upon a majestic steamboat that sailed up the mighty Mississippi River. We spent a good twenty-four hours upon this vessel, and once we reached the shore, we settled into a camp for a day or two. It was at this encampment that a small incident occurred, causing quite a stir among our company. One of our young girls, a sixteen-year-old miss named Miss Pressley, ventured down to the river's edge to fetch a pail of water. Unfortunately, her footing betrayed her, leading to a sudden plunge into the water's depths. Were it not for the swift actions of a nearby gentleman who leapt in and came to her rescue, she would have met a watery demise.

Having left that camp behind, we boarded another train to proceed with our westward voyage. After traversing the lands for approximately twenty-four hours, we arrived at the banks of the Missouri River. A new steamboat awaited us there, ready to carry us along the Missouri's currents. Our disembarkation occurred in a humble town by the name of Wymore, nestled within the borders of Nebraska. Upon setting foot on its soil, we discovered a vast encampment of English and Scandinavian immigrants eagerly anticipating teams of oxen from Utah. These teams would transport the pilgrims to Zion, as the majority of these individuals lacked the means to procure their own provisions for the arduous journey.

Contrary to their circumstances, the families accompanying us from Africa possessed a fair amount of wealth and were able to acquire their own supplies. Here, at this very place, my fifteen-year-old brother, John, bid us farewell. He secured employment under a man named Ramsey, who required his services as a mule team driver on the road to Salt Lake City. Remarkably, he reached his destination ahead of the rest of our group.

Regrettably, I recall that among these less fortunate immigrants who had been awaiting their departure for several weeks, an outbreak of cholera emerged, claiming the lives of numerous souls.

In the meantime, my mother and her four children partook in a baptismal ceremony within the Missouri River, thereby joining the ranks of the Church of Jesus Christ of Latter Day Saints.

Well, dear reader, let me take you on a journey back to a time when dreams and debts danced hand in hand, and a river's embrace could both give and take away.

Now, picture this, a place far from Utah's golden valleys, where the church's heartbeats resided. It was a time when oxen teams were as rare as a diamond in a haystack, a precious thing that needed chasing. So, the church's agent that accompanied us from the city of New York, he decided to beckon the shadows of debt, believing it wise to do so. This debt, it wasn't some dark cloud, but rather a lantern lighting the way. It was to buy oxen, yokes, chains, and wagons, a convoy of hope that would carry the pioneers forward.

But let me tell you, life's tapestry isn't woven without some tangles. Here's a tale, as vivid as the summer's sun, of a lad named Jim, a mere ten years young. He met the Missouri River in a tumble, swift currents playing with him like a puppet on a string. Downstream he drifted, like a leaf dancing on the water's rhythm. But just when it seemed like the river was to be his fate, fortune whispered in the language of a worn log. It jutted from the water's embrace like a guardian angel, and with strength that only the young possess, Jim clung to it. Like a lifeline thrown by fate itself. And there, in that river's embrace, he clung to that log as if it was his oldest friend. But fear not, for family is like a lighthouse in a storm. His kin, they dashed onto that log like heroes in a tale, extending their hands to pull him from the river's embrace.

And so, as the river flowed, time flowed too. Oxen, they were sought, from wherever they could be found. And most, they were steers untrained, wild as the wind and as unpredictable as the stars in the night sky. Oh, what an adventure it was, what a merry dance it became. You see, these folks, they knew not the ways of cattle, especially the Scandinavians, far from their home shores. They stared at these creatures as if they were myths sprung to life, their appearance unfamiliar as a stranger's face.

But listen close, for every tale has its threads of experience. For I, I had some knowledge in this art of managing these creatures, thanks to my own past, my father's reliance on oxen back in the lands of Africa. And so, when the time came, when these oxen were assigned to me, I stood with a heart full of confidence. I could rope 'em like a true cowboy, and in no time, I mastered the art of yoking them, like a conductor guiding a grand orchestra. Three yokes of oxen, they were mine, and they became a part of my world. For three days, we danced this dance, me and my oxen, practicing the steps before our grand westward journey.

And so, my friends, as the sun sets on this tale, remember that debts can be lanterns guiding us to dreams, rivers can be both givers and takers, and life, oh life, it's a journey where even the most unfamiliar creatures can become companions. And sometimes, just sometimes, it's the knowledge we carry, the experiences we hold, that can turn even the wildest steers into a mirthful adventure, a dance under the open sky of destiny.

Vividly do I recall the morning of our departure. Who would lead this thousand-mile expedition? Each teamster, whip in hand, their wagons already hitched, eagerly awaited the captain's command to commence our march. On the first day, a Scandinavian took the lead, supported by men walking alongside the cattle to ensure they stayed on the designated path. Thus, we set forth. Our caravan consisted of between 150 and 200 wagons, and we covered a remarkable ten miles of our thousand-mile journey that very first day.

As night fell, some of us unyoked our cattle, while others left them harnessed, fearful that they might struggle to be yoked again if freed. A group of men stood guard that night, preventing the cattle from straying. We also fortified our camp with a protective perimeter. Most of us, weary from the day's toils, managed to find a restful slumber.

Now, gather 'round, my brothers and sisters, for the sun has dipped below the horizon, and the stars are our companions in this tale. The day has been long, the air carries the scent of toil, but the fire in our hearts still burns bright.

As the morning light kissed the sky, the land came alive with the sounds of rustling cattle, their hooves drumming a rhythm of life. We gathered, hungry bellies aching for sustenance, and devoured a hearty breakfast, filling our bellies for the journey ahead. With the taste of food in our mouths and the promise of a new day, our spirits soared like birds taking flight.

But let me tell you, my friends, this day was no easy stroll through a field of daisies. It was a rugged path, an arduous march that tested the very mettle of our souls. The oxen, bless their hearts, grew weary as the sun began its climb, their strength bowing to the weight of the wagon's dreams. And so, we called an early halt, setting up camp as the golden sun dipped towards the western horizon.

But oh, the night, it had surprises in store. Our captain, Minor G. Atwood, a man of spirit and heart, called upon those who possessed fiddles to step forth. And lo and behold, as the fiddles began their lively tunes, something magical happened. Like leaves in a whirlwind, the majority of us were caught up in a spontaneous dance, a prairie dance beneath the watchful gaze of the stars.

And when weariness began to flirt with our bones, the captain gathered us like a shepherd gathering his flock. With earnestness in his eyes, he spoke words of wisdom that danced like fireflies in the night. He spoke of righteousness, of walking this path with hearts filled with goodness, invoking the blessings of the Divine upon our humble camp. He promised that as long as our spirits stood tall and our hearts remained resolute, we would carve our journey through the tapestry of destiny, and happiness would be our reward.

And so, under the vast canopy of stars, voices rose like hymns, harmonizing with the whispers of the night wind. Hymns of Zion, songs that tethered us to our faith, filled the air. And then, in the silence that followed, a brother among us, moved by the currents of devotion, stepped forth. He offered a prayer, his words weaving a tapestry of guidance and protection, a plea to the Almighty to guide our footsteps through the

30

uncharted territories.

The captain, oh his wisdom, he painted the path that lay ahead. He spoke of challenges as rugged as the earth beneath our feet, of disappointments that may bloom like thorns in our journey. He acknowledged the specter of cholera, a grim companion that haunted our ranks. And with a heavy heart, he cautioned that some may be called to lay down their lives as offerings to this journey.

And so, my dear readers, as we lay down in our makeshift beds, let the stars be our witnesses, the wind our lullaby. For we are a caravan of souls, a tapestry woven with courage and faith, marching into the unknown, where challenges are companions, and each step is a verse in the ballad of our destiny.

Shortly before embarking on this thousand-mile odyssey, we encountered a widow, Mrs. Gibbet, and her young daughter, Susan. Lacking means of transportation, they found refuge in our wagon, with the provision that they provided their own sustenance. As our westward journey progressed, the captain developed a fondness for the young maiden, ultimately leading to their marriage in Salt Lake City.

Things went reasonably well, though our oxen and the pilgrims would grow weary and fatigued. We managed to cover approximately twelve miles each day, occasionally fifteen when we needed to push a bit farther to reach water.

Now, dear readers, as we journey through the heart of the land, where rivers flow like the tales of old and mountains rise like the spirits of the ancestors.

As we tread the land of Nebraska, a land that stretches wide like the embrace of a long-lost friend, we came upon the Platt River. A ribbon of water cutting through the earth, it lay in wait for us to cross. But let me tell you, this river, it wasn't just a gentle ride across. It held treacherous secrets in the form of quicksands, lurking beneath its surface. These treacherous traps played tricks on us, making it as arduous as a dance on a stormy night to guide our train across. Oh, those quicksands, they tested our spirits, but we forged on, determined to conquer their tricks.

But wait, my friends, that wasn't the only challenge nature had in store for us. Mosquitoes, oh how they swarmed like an army of invisible foes, tormenting both man and beast. Their bites, like relentless drumbeats, tormented us to the edge of our endurance. And the cattle, bless their hearts, they weren't spared either. Tormented beyond bearing, they stampeded, their hooves thundering like the drums of nature's rebellion. It took us hours, hours like the tick of a clock, to gather them back, to bring harmony to this dance of chaos.

And as the sun set and rose, the cycle of life and death continued. Each day, we bid farewell to companions, souls who had walked with us through the twists and turns of this journey. But onward we pressed, our spirits unwavering, our hearts a mixture of sorrow and determination. My team, spirited and swift, often stayed behind as the caravan moved on. With me stood a guard of fellow souls, and together we performed the solemn duty of burying our fallen comrades. Sometimes it was one, sometimes two, three, four, even five individuals a day. Sewn up in simple sheets, they were laid to rest in a common grave, a reminder of the fragility of life and the strength of unity. Before we resumed our march, a voice among us would offer a prayer, a dedication of hope and remembrance, a moment to honor those who had parted ways with this world.

And as the land stretched further, mountains rising like sentinels on the horizon, another challenge emerged. Mountain fever, a specter that threatened to steal the life from my own brother, Jim. Days stretched like endless paths, his health hanging in the balance. But listen closely, for faith is a fire that burns even in the darkest nights. Our mother, a pillar of unwavering conviction, she believed in a miracle. Elders among us, their hands anointed with oil, they offered prayers like songs to the heavens, seeking divine intervention. Just as the shadow of despair grew heavy, hope whispered its secrets. Signs of recovery appeared, like the first rays of dawn after a long, dark night. Jim, he fought, he held on, and he emerged victorious, a testament to the resilience of the human spirit.

And so, my friends, as we stand on the threshold of the unknown, remember this tale. Remember that rivers hold secrets, challenges carve paths, and faith, oh faith, it's the light that guides us through the darkest nights. As we journey, as we press on through the trials of life, let the memory of those who walked before us be our guiding star, and may their stories, like whispers on the wind, inspire us to face each new dawn with courage and grace.

As our caravan wove its way through this wild expanse, we came across a few souls who had known these lands long before us, the Indians. They were like whispers in the wind, scarce and fleeting, leaving us with a sense of mystery in their wake. And oh, the buffalo, those majestic creatures who roamed the land like kings. From a distance, we caught glimpses of them, a reminder of the wild heart that still beat in this untamed world.

Yet, it wasn't just the buffalo that shared this realm with us. The antelope, they danced across the land in numbers too great to count. But oh, sometimes even beauty can be a thorn in the side. These antelope, they thrived like a river in the rain, but their feasting ways left our cattle wanting. They devoured the grass, like a banquet they couldn't resist, leaving behind a scarcity that echoed through the land. The cattle, they depended on that grass, and so we found ourselves in a dance, a dance between survival and sharing.

But onward we pressed, for the journey wasn't just a stroll through a garden. It was a rugged path, a road that tested both man and beast. We trudged through swampy terrains, where mosquitoes swarmed like a fury. But as the old saying goes, storms eventually settle, and so did our journey. The rhythm of oxen's hooves, like a song sung by the land, carried us forward. Twelve, fifteen miles a day, like the heartbeat of a determined dreamer, we moved steadily.

But, alas, my friends, the journey wasn't without its sorrows. The dreaded bloody murrain, a name that sounds like a curse whispered by the wind, it befell our cattle. A malady that stole their strength, their vitality, like a shadow creeping over a flame. And what was the cause, you ask? The very water they drank, laced with alkali's bitterness. Like a poison, it coursed through their veins, and we could only watch, hearts heavy with helplessness.

And so, my dear souls, as we tread through these tales of old, let the winds of the past carry these stories to your hearts. For in these whispers of time, you'll find the echoes of a journey, a journey that painted both the beauty and the challenges of a land waiting to be conquered. And in each challenge, in each triumph, may you see the reflection of the human spirit, the spirit that marched, that danced, that endured, and that, against all odds, pressed on like a river to the sea.

You see, on this path of ours, all the souls who relied on the church for their travel, they had to travel by foot and walk. A humble parade of determined dedicated believers, trudging forward through dusty paths. Even the teamsters, those who guided the wagons through this quilt of earth, they too were foot-bound. But in the midst of this sea of walkers, a special sight stood out like a gem in the sand.

It was my mother, you see, a woman of her own kind. She had her own team, a pair of steady oxen who pulled our wagon's weight. And she and the children, they rode in that wagon. As for me, well, I walked beside our oxen like a guardian spirit. With each step, we moved forward, a family bound by hope and a future yet untold.

But oh, my friends, life's road is a twisted one, and sometimes, a twist of fate can turn joy into sorrow. One day, when the sun was warm on our shoulders and the horizon seemed to stretch forever, our cattle, they stampeded like the echoes of a forgotten thunderstorm. The wagons, the hooves, all in a wild dance, and then, like a fragile leaf crushed underfoot, tragedy struck. A young woman, like a blooming rose cut in its prime, trampled to her death. Why, you ask? No soul could say, for the cause of that stampede, like a ghost, remained unseen.

And if that was not enough, fate had yet another cruel card to play. In the darkness of the night, a girl, she danced with danger as she fried the meat. But fire, it's a beast that doesn't heed the call of man. It leaped, it danced, and it caught her clothes in its fiery grip. Panic, like a storm, swept through her, and she flung the blazing pan away, but the fire had already kissed her skin. She ran, oh how she ran, until arms reached out to stop her. But the damage was done, for her skin was charred and her fate was sealed. She endured, she suffered, but in the morning's light, she left this world.

And then came a day, a day etched in memory like a scar on the heart. A midday pause, a break from the journey, a chance to breathe in the air of the land. We corralled the wagons, unharnessed the cattle, ready to let them graze by the Platt River. But then, like a sudden storm, the air filled with war cries, with the fierce spirits of the land itself. Indians, they emerged like phantoms from a grove of cottonwoods. They came with shouts and arrows, with rifles in hand. In that moment, we realized how ill-prepared we were. Guns lay in the wagons, out of reach, and only a handful of us carried arms. But pride swelled within me, a young soul with a revolver in hand. Bang, bang, bang, my shots echoed like cries in the wilderness, but I could never say if they found their mark.

The cattle, oh they sensed the chaos, their agitation a dance of fear. Yet some among us were quick, and they drove the cattle back into their makeshift pen. The Indians circled, like wolves on a prowl, encircling us with their war cries. Twice, they circled, their yells a deafening storm, and when they were done, nine of our men were left wounded. Some among us, they lagged behind, stumbling back from the world's edge, unaware of the battle that raged. And the Indians, they seized this moment, like a hawk swooping on its prey. A woman, lassoed like a wild mare, they carried her away on horseback, a prize of their conquest.

And so, there we stood, caught in the clutches of confusion and grief. The woman gone, her husband wounded, and the night whispered its secrets of uncertainty. The captain, a pillar of wisdom and strength, he called together a gathering of strong souls, men whose hearts beat with courage. They weighed the paths before them, the possibilities and perils. To chase the Indians, a cry for vengeance, it was a tempting call. But reason won over fury, for the path was fraught with danger. Leaving the camp meant leaving our women and children vulnerable, a risk that was too great to take.

And so, my dear hearts, as we gather 'round this fire, let the winds of the past carry these tales to your ears. For in these whispers of time, you'll find the echoes of bravery, the shadows of loss, and the choices that shaped a journey across the heart of this land. And as you listen, may you carry these stories with you, as lanterns to guide your own path, and may they remind you that every step taken in the dance of life holds within it the power to change destinies and shape the very tapestry of our existence.

The captain's voice cut through the air like a trumpet call, firm and unwavering. "Hitch up, yoke the wagons," he declared, and like a well-practiced symphony, we followed his command. The land stretched before us, rolling hills reaching out like the hands of old friends. We marched, wheels creaking like an ancient song, until evening's shroud wrapped around us. Ah, my friends, when the sun dipped low, it was as if the world held its breath, waiting for the night's secrets to unfold.

And unfold they did, as we carved our camp from the earth itself. Wagons formed a circle like a ring of old friends, the corral for our four-legged companions. Cattle unharnessed, we guarded them like knights guarding a sacred relic. The captain's voice held sway once again, "No fires," he commanded, and so the night lay draped in a blanket of darkness. Those who had thought ahead, their bellies tasted warmth as they feasted on their pre-prepared meals. But for many, hunger was a constant companion, an empty chair at our campfire.

The morning came, as it always does, chasing away the night's terrors with its golden embrace. But the dawn brought its own sorrows. Three cattle, like shadows of their former selves, lay still, victims of hunger's cruel embrace. Ah, the pains of the journey, etched in the bones of both man and beast. And so, with heavy hearts, we moved on, the cattle's weary steps echoing our own exhaustion.

But fate, my friends, she's a fickle mistress. As the day's journey drew us like a moth to a flame, a water source emerged, like a gift from the heavens. The cattle, oh they drank, their parched throats finding solace. And us, the travelers, we cast our burdens aside for a moment, granting ourselves the luxury of rest. We settled there for the day, as if the world itself had decided to give us a respite. The oxen, they lounged like kings, their weary eyes finding solace in the shade. We posted guards, for even in a moment of rest, we knew the land's secrets could turn against us.

The night came, my friends, and it came like a gentle whisper. But in its whispers, we heard the rustle of leaves, the secrets of the earth. Signs of Indians, their marks on the land like footprints in the snow. We braced ourselves for an onslaught, every heartbeat a drumroll of anticipation. But, as the night deepened, relief emerged like a clearing storm. The attack never came, the night remained quiet, and our camp remained our own.

The next morning, after our much-needed rest, we set out early. We knew that Fort Laramie was just a short distance away, and we were eager to report the disappearance of the woman to the authorities at the fort. We arrived at the fort that night, hoping it would alleviate our troubles. Instead, our troubles multiplied as the fort officer and his soldiers came to our camp. They demanded the release of certain women, claiming they had been coerced into journeying to Salt Lake against their will. They informed us of receiving a telegram from the East, instructing them to search our camp.

Our captain spoke up, saying, "Gentlemen, we are willing to allow you to search the camp. However, only the officer and two of his men may enter, while the rest must remain outside. But we shall do even better than that—I will gather our congregation together." Thus, our captain had the bugler sound the call, summoning the people to assemble. Men, women, and children came forth, and the captain relayed the officer's message about the alleged forced travel to Utah. He said, "If any among you are being compelled to journey to Utah against your will, or if any are weary of traveling with us and wish to remain behind, show it by raising your right hand."

Not a solitary hand was raised. Our captain then addressed the officer, saying, "Are you contented?" The officer retorted, "No, I am not, for I suspect that you have concealed some women in your encampment, and we desire to conduct a search." "Very well," responded our captain, "you and two of your men may inspect the camp, examine every wagon, but your soldiers must remain outside." Our captain appointed a guard to ensure that the soldiers were kept at bay.

These men scrutinized the wagons, and upon finding no one, they interrogated many of the women. However, all of them expressed their desire to remain with us. Due to the soldiers' animosity, our captain deemed it unwise to divulge anything about our skirmishes with the Indians or the woman's capture. Consequently, the next morning, we resumed our journey, all feeling content that our circumstances were as favorable as they were.

Well, gather 'round once more, my friends, and let me take you on a journey through hills and rivers, through the dance of rain and snow, where the world itself seemed to whisper secrets in the wind.

The land rose and fell like a symphony, its melodies written in the shape of hills. Our wagons, like determined ants, moved forward at a slower pace. For the hills, they taught us patience, they taught us the value of steady steps. Raindrops fell like blessings from above, their pitter-patter a rhythm to our steps. And as we entered the embrace of the hilly country, a familiar companion returned to us—the Platt River, known by the name "The Three Crossings." Here, the river's flow mirrored our own journey, winding through the land like a silver ribbon.

But it wasn't just the river that greeted us. No, my friends, it was something more magical than a river's song. It was snow, descending from the heavens like a gift from the gods. A snowstorm, a symphony of white, and as the flakes kissed the earth, it felt like a painting come to life. Oh, how the world transformed under that snowy blanket, like a new chapter of creation itself.

To me, that snow, it held a kind of magic. But as time waltzed on, that magic began to change. The cold, it crept in, wrapping around us like an icy embrace. For souls like me, who hailed from warmer lands, that cold, it was a new kind of challenge. Yet, even as the snowflakes fell like frozen stars, there was a beauty in their dance, a reminder that even in the harshest of moments, there's still a touch of wonder.

And then, the snow's dance ceased, and light emerged once more, banishing the shadows. But oh, those nights, they clung to the chill, wrapping themselves around us like a cloak of frost. Yet, the days, they still held the promise of warmth, the promise of progress.

Ah, my friends, the journey led us to the Green River, a force of nature that cut through the land like a scar. And there, in the midst of a snowstorm, we faced the challenge of fording that river. But by the grace of fate or providence, we managed to cross, the wagons like brave ships battling the storm. And as the night draped its velvety curtain over the world, we settled, grateful for the shelter of our wagons and the warmth of our campfires.

Devil's Slide, a name that echoed like a whisper in the breeze, marked the path's descent. Like a river finding its way back to the sea, our journey descended through that slide, a dance of wagon wheels on the path. And there, like a bird returning to its nest, my brother Joseph joined us. A reunion, like a balm for the soul, for he had walked this path before, a guide in this unfamiliar land.

And as we move forward, my dear listeners, remember that even through hills and rivers, through the trials of snow and cold, the journey's twists and turns are the threads that weave the tapestry of our lives. And in these tales, may you find the strength to face your own challenges, the wisdom to embrace the beauty in every moment, and the joy of reunion when paths once again converge.

Joseph advised Mother to abandon the train, as their progress was so slow that he estimated they would not reach their destination until late November, at the earliest. Our captain opposed the idea and urged us to remain with the train. However, brother Joseph convinced Mother to forge ahead, disregarding our captain's counsel.

Thus, we bid farewell to our captain and all our companions with whom we had journeyed for many months. We embarked alone, with a single wagon and three teams of oxen. The widow and her daughter, who had traveled with us in our wagon, chose to stay with the train. Therefore, Mother, my brothers Joseph and Jim, my sister Mary Ann, and I set out to complete the remainder of the journey unaccompanied. We made steady progress, but only managed to outpace the train by a mere two days.

One evening remains vivid in my memory. At twilight, as we emerged from Emigration Canyon onto the plain, the lights of Salt Lake City came into view before us. What a magnificent sight it was! The street lamps and the lights shining from the windows of homes were the first illuminations we had beheld in nearly four months. We drove to the home of dear friends, who had been our neighbors in Africa. They provided us with comfort and even encouraged us to stay in Salt Lake. However, we deemed it impossible, as brother Joe had already established his place in Glenwood near Payson, further south, and was eager to continue the next morning.

With our cattle weary, fatigued, and partially ailing, we could only cover a few miles each day. It took us approximately four days to reach Payson, situated around sixty miles south of Salt Lake. Along the way, another wagon joined us at Salt Lake, bound for Glenwood. When we arrived in Payson, we spent a night with another friend from Africa, who attempted to persuade us to settle there. Nevertheless, we pressed on.

As we departed Payson, one of our oxen succumbed completely, so we exchanged it for a gun. A few days later, another ox met its demise.

Our subsequent stop was Santiquin. As we neared Santiquin, the remaining oxen grew so exhausted that they veered off the road, eager to make camp. I endeavored to guide them back onto the road when suddenly, a woman appeared seemingly out of nowhere, waving at me and shouting  desperately, "What are you doing on top of my house?" Thus,

I was introduced to my first encounter with a dugout. The revelation that people dwelt in a hole in the ground shocked me, but as the winter wore on, I became well acquainted with such abodes.

After leaving Santiquin, our next halt was Nephi. From Nephi onward, the population grew increasingly scarce. After Nephi, we encountered a camp at Fayette, and from there, we proceeded to Salina. Once we departed Salina, we had to cross the Sevier River at a location called Rocky Ford. Several days prior, a man had been slain by Indians at Rocky Ford, and we received advice to postpone our journey until a larger party could join us. However, our longing to reach our destination propelled us forward.

We were exceedingly weary, yet remained vigilant. As we reached the middle of the stream, our oxen balked, compelling one of us to wade into the water and drive them across. I was chosen to undertake this task. Though the water was not very deep, it was bitterly cold, but I managed to urge the oxen across the ford.

We feared that the oxen may have sensed the danger posed by the Indians, causing their hesitation. Nevertheless, we successfully crossed and continued onward to Glenwood. My eldest brother William greeted us roughly two miles outside of Glenwood. I vividly recall William climbing into the wagon to embrace Mother, and the tears of joy that welled in her eyes upon being reunited with her eldest sons, knowing she was now near the culmination of her journey. Finally, close to midnight, we reached our destination, and William's wife had prepared a hearty meal for us. We rested for four

or five days in his abode, after which my brother suggested that if Mother intended to settle there, she should explore the area and find a dwelling of her own.

We discovered a plot of land in the small town of Glenwood, near Richfield, comprising approximately an acre, accompanied by a one-room dugout. The acreage was fenced, and we believed it would serve as a splendid spot to build a home. Mother purchased the property and settled into the dugout.

We acquired 25 bushels of wheat, which William and I loaded onto our wagon and transported to Manti. As it was now December, the weather was bitterly cold, yet the ground remained devoid of snow. We unloaded the wheat at the mill and camped there while the miller ground our grain. At that time, it was the sole mill in the county, drawing inhabitants from distances of up to one hundred miles who sought to have their wheat milled.

That evening, as we gathered around the fireplace, preparing our suppers, a considerable crowd of men had congregated, their bowie knives and revolvers conspicuously hanging from their belts, engrossed in discussions about Indian troubles. One of the men, cooking meat, allowed the grease to catch fire. In his haste, he grabbed the pan from the flames, scorching his hands to the point where he dropped it on the floor. I sat nearby, and as the pan struck the ground, the scalding meat and grease were propelled into the air, colliding with my face. Everyone was eager to assist me, expressing deep remorse for the accident, yet no one knew how to alleviate the pain. I endured considerable agony, but the miller suggested applying flour to my face to soothe the burns, claiming it would draw out the heat. They covered my face in flour and wrapped a sack around it. I suffered greatly that night, but I believe the flour aided in cooling my face and relieving the pain. The following morning, our ground grain was ready. My brother loaded it onto the wagon, along with myself, and we embarked for home. The journey was fraught with intense cold, and we encountered difficulties crossing the rocky ford due to ice. Nevertheless, we arrived home on the second day after departing from the mill.

Upon my arrival at home, my dear mother tenderly removed the plaster from my face, uncovering a dreadful burn. Swollen and raw, my countenance bore the marks of agony. It was then, in that moment of revelation, that I discovered my sight had abandoned me. With no doctor to be found in our humble community, it fell upon Mother's caring hands to do what she could. Despair loomed over us, casting a shadow upon our hopes for my vision. Yet, in a matter of days, a glimmer of sight returned to one eye, and in due time, both eyes regained their function. Throughout the winter, I was confined to the shelter of our home, my face a constant reminder of the ordeal I had endured. But when spring finally graced us with its presence, I could venture outside, engaging in the modest tasks of chopping wood and tending to our modest garden.

It was in the wintry month of January, back in 1866, that I celebrated my thirteenth birthday within the confines of a dugout. Nevertheless, Mother's loving touch graced the occasion with a homemade birthday cake, a sweet testament to her unwavering devotion.

With the arrival of spring in the year 1866, life took on a new rhythm, a rhythm of preparation and creation. The land, kissed by the sun's warmth, seemed to beckon us to till its soil and bring forth life. And so, we busied ourselves, our hands turning the earth, planting seeds that would become our sustenance. But as the days unfurled, so did our plans for a new dwelling, a shelter woven from dreams and sweat. A house, a sanctuary, rising from the ground like a phoenix from the ashes.

And then came that March day, like any other day, as the sun cast its golden glow upon the land. We ventured into the mountains, our wagons creaking like old friends in conversation. But then, like a distant thunder, the sound of a bass drum reached our ears. Oh, my friends, it was no tune of celebration, but a somber rhythm, a warning whispered by the wind itself. Indians, their presence lurking in the hills like shadows.

Six of us, a brave band with our four teams, stood still as the wind carried those haunting drums to our ears. A rider, swift as the wind itself, passed by, a messenger of urgency, bearing news of Indian danger. With hearts heavy, we turned our teams, our oxen understanding the urgency in their very bones. As we hurried back towards town, a man's resolve shone like a distant star, unyielding against the fear that gripped us. He turned back for his team, a decision that sealed his fate.

Days unfolded their story, and that man, he never returned to our campfire's light. The dawn revealed a cruel truth, a truth etched in the blood-soaked earth—a life lost, a scalp claimed. The Indians, like ghosts, had visited him in the night, leaving only sorrow in their wake. A warning to us all, a harsh lesson in the art of survival.

And so, the Indians, they remained a specter in the distance, a constant threat that danced at the edges of our days. They came, not as friends, but as shadows of danger, attacking ranchers and travelers who dared tread the roads. Our once peaceful settlement, it became a place of unease, of anxious glances cast over shoulders, of doors locked tight against the night's fears.

In the end, my friends, our humble homes, built with care and love, became vulnerable under the weight of danger. And so, we took our courage in hand and left behind those homes, seeking refuge in the embrace of a larger community. Richfield, with its safety in numbers, became our new haven, a sanctuary from the storm that was the Indian threat.

May these tales remind you, dear reader, that life's rhythms are ever-changing, a symphony of joy and sorrow. And in these stories, may you find the strength to face the unknown, the wisdom to make difficult choices, and the hope that even in the darkest of times, there is a community, a place of safety and solace, waiting to embrace you.

Thus, in April of 1866, we bid farewell to our humble dugout and made our way to Richfield. Though a mere three miles separated us from our former abode, some of the men would periodically return to Glenwood to tend to their farming duties. As the autumn harvest approached, most of the people began to trickle back to their homes, for the Indian raids had ceased with the arrival of winter. During this time, Mother made the decision to relocate to Cache Valley, to a small settlement near Logan. Arriving in the fall, we were just in time to scythe and stack hay on the prairie, where we camped in our wagon until enough logs were gathered to erect a modest log house measuring 14 by 16 feet. It was then that we finally felt a sense of security, as the Indians showed no interest in troubling the people of that area.

Once our humble abode was complete and a corral had been built, we received a letter from our brother William expressing his desire to join us in our newfound haven. Consequently, my brother John and I returned to Glenwood to assist William Henry in his relocation. It was during our time there, in the month of March 1867, that Joseph ventured out into the meadow, in search of a heifer expected to give birth. Seated, he patiently awaited the arrival of two men descending from the Richfield mountain. However, as they drew nearer, it became clear that they were Indians. Joseph, sensing imminent danger, sprang to his feet and raced towards town, while the Indians crouched low, taking aim at him. Fortunately, he managed to reach safety, narrowly escaping the whistling bullets that followed in his wake. Immediately, he alerted the townsfolk, and the solemn beat of the drums resounded once more.

Meanwhile, a band of Indians emerged from over the ridge, gathering cattle from the meadow and driving them into King's Meadow Canyon. As the men of our settlement assembled, armed with their guns, my brother Joe was entrusted with the task of carrying news of the raid to Richfield. Along his journey, at the crossing of the Severe River, he discovered the lifeless bodies of two men and a woman—a grim testament to the Indians' brutality. Urgently, he continued to Richfield, informing the populace of the raids.

The men, determined to intercept and deter the Indians, ascended the mountain ridge, only to find the red men lying in wait, concealed beneath the brow of the hill. As we crested the hill, they unleashed their volleys, one of which found its mark in my brother John. The bullet pierced his arm, tore through his right side, and exited from his back. Our captain swiftly ordered us to take cover behind rocks and trees, and we retaliated with a relentless hail of bullets upon the Indians.

A midst this chaotic skirmish, John's strength began to wane, and he felt the onset of dizziness. Blood trickled down his side, marking the extent of his injury. At that moment, the captain instructed an elderly man named "Susie" and me to escort him back to town. Despite his considerable loss of blood, John summoned the strength to walk the distance. With the aid of compassionate sisters, we tended to his wounds, dressing them and providing solace. Over time, his condition improved, and he eventually made a full recovery.

Our brave men refused to pursue the Indians into the canyon, but my brother William and another valiant soul volunteered to retrieve our stolen cattle. Though many deemed it foolhardy, their determination drove them to attempt the impossible. After two days and nights, they returned with approximately half of our precious herd.

In response to the Indian threat, the Territorial Government dispatched a contingent from the North to safeguard the settlers in the South. When they arrived in Glenwood, a council meeting was convened, and a resolution was passed deeming it perilous for anyone to venture into the canyons, as the Indians would undoubtedly lie in wait, ready to annihilate our boys. And so, the protective contingent returned to the North.

It took two weeks before brother John's condition stabilized enough for him to be moved. At that juncture, we bid Glenwood farewell, embarking on a journey to Cache Valley. Once there, I spent the next four months immersed in logging work, which proved to be a reasonably profitable endeavor. We secured a small farm on lease and cultivated a modest crop of corn, potatoes, and wheat. The harvest proved bountiful, and during that time, my brother Joe penned a letter from Payson, informing us of a new frontier and an eight-mile canal under construction. Eager for fresh opportunities, we resolved to relocate there. As autumn drew near and we gathered the fruits of our labor, selling some of our produce, Mother, John, Jim, and my sister departed for Payson, while I remained behind to complete the harvesting.

When Mother reached Payson, she purchased a lot with a two-room log house on it. The family found contentment in their new abode, and they implored me to sell our property in Cache Valley and join them in Payson. Fortunately, I managed to trade it for a yoke of oxen and a wagon.

And so, I gathered the remaining grain and loaded it onto the wagon, along with the remaining household belongings. With a heavy heart, I bid farewell to Cache Valley. It was late in the fall of 1867 when I set off early in the morning, hoping to cover considerable ground and reach the small town of Copenhagen in Wellsville Canyon by nightfall. The path was treacherously uphill, and my wagon was laden with a substantial load that taxed the strength of the oxen, allowing only for incremental progress. As I neared the summit, disaster struck—the chain snapped, and the wagon careened backward down the hill. Seizing the brake, I clung to it for dear life, hurtling some hundred feet before the wagon finally came to a halt, its tongue pointing precariously downward. Once I had the oxen back in harness, I realized the chain had broken, prompting me to fashion a makeshift repair using a sagebrush. I commenced my ascent up the hill for the second time, and this time fortune favored me.

From thereon, the journey was downhill through the canyon. By the time I reached Copenhagen, I made camp on the outskirts of town, unyoked the oxen, and settled in for the night. The following morning, after a restful sleep, I discovered my oxen had wandered off a short distance. I corralled them back into camp, enjoyed a hearty breakfast, and resumed my descent through the canyon. Progress came more easily now that my load was significantly lighter, and shortly before noon, I arrived in Box Elder. That night, I found lodging in a small settlement this side of Farmington, where a friend of my sister had been staying. My sister joined me there, and the next day, we resumed our journey, arriving in Salt Lake City before noon. To lighten my burden, I exchanged the grain at the tithing office for an order that I could redeem upon reaching Payson. I sought out our old friend Henry Dixon, who had made his home with my father in Africa during his missionary work there. When Henry converted to the Mormon faith, his father disinherited him, forsaking a vast inheritance to remain true to his beliefs. Henry extended his utmost hospitality to my sister and me, providing a warm and welcoming refuge for the night. The following morning, after a hearty breakfast, we set out for Payson, making swift progress with our reduced load. Three days after leaving Salt Lake City, we arrived in Payson, our journey at an end.

Upon my arrival, the first soul to greet my weary eyes was a sprightly lad by the name of Staheli. He kindly pointed me toward my mother's humble abode. Fate, with its whimsical ways, wove our destinies together. In the course of a few years, Staheli and I found ourselves bound in matrimony, for we had the fortune of marrying sisters. Thus, a bond of friendship was forged between us, a bond that would weather the trials of time.

The embrace of home filled me with gladness, for I knew it to be a lasting haven. My dear mother, till the end of her days, resided in Payson, a testament to the constancy of our dwelling.

As the winter winds of 1867 whispered through the canyons, we toiled like ants beneath the sun's gaze. Days stretched out like a quilt, stitched together with our labor. Timber, strong and sturdy, was hewn from the heart of the land, fences were erected to cradle the promise of prosperity, and our homestead began to wear the cloak of adornment. Oh, how we poured our sweat and dreams into that dwelling, crafting it not just as a shelter but as a testament to our hopes.

And then, as the sun danced higher in the sky, as the snows melted like dreams awakening, spring arrived in all its splendor. With the birth of spring, a new chapter unfolded for us. A lease was secured, a plot of land now known as Benjamin District, nestled just six miles from our abode. With hearts brimming with anticipation, we pitched our camp there, like pioneers staking their claim on a world of possibility.

Our hands, like magic wands, transformed the earth. Seven acres of fertile soil stretched before us, and with every step we took, hope was sown. Wheat, barley, and potatoes, like promises from the soil itself, were carefully placed in the embrace of the earth. The land accepted our offerings, and we tended to it with diligence and care. With every ray of sunlight, with every drop of rain, the earth responded, and our crops thrived. The promise of harvest, of abundance, it hung in the air like the sweetest melody.

But ah, my friends, even as the world blossomed around us, a shadow began to darken our dreams. The locusts, those voracious creatures, descended upon our fields like a plague. The land, once so promising, became a battleground, a place of despair. These insects, like hungry spirits, devoured all in their path. The fields, once lush and green, turned to desolation under their ravenous hunger.

And so, those crops that had promised us sustenance and success, they withered beneath the onslaught of the locusts' gluttony. Wheat, barley, potatoes—all were swallowed by the earth, leaving behind only the bitter taste of loss. Our hopes, like fragile petals, were scattered by the winds of misfortune.

But even in the face of such adversity, my friends, we must remember that the cycle of life is a dance of both triumph and defeat. For just as the locusts took, so too shall the land give once more. With every fall of seed, with every turn of the seasons, hope is rekindled, and dreams are resurrected. And in these stories, may you find the strength to weather the storms, the patience to endure the hardships, and the resilience to rise again, just as the land itself does, year after year.

During the ensuing winter, we toiled on the Salem Irrigation Canal. This mighty canal, stretching eight miles in length, was hewn by hand, pick, and shovel, its path surveyed by a "spirit level" to ascertain its descent. In the grip of two winters, we toiled amidst ice and snow, subsisting mostly on bread and molasses. Nay, there were naysayers who sought to dissuade our spirits, claiming that the waters would never flow once the canal stood complete, for the very essence of physics would defy their course uphill.

A fellowship known as the ANME of The Salem Irrigation Canal Company took shape. It comprised settlers hailing from Payson and Salem, united by the notion of drawing lots for their lands. Each man, guided by his fateful draw, selected plots spanning five or ten acres. My brother Joseph, having attained his majority and having entered wedlock, laid claim to five acres. My other sibling, John, found himself the steward of ten acres, while I, in honor of my mother, secured ten acres as well.

We commenced our labor, plowing the earth and tending to the grains destined to adorn the summer's bounty. Two and a half acres of wheat, a like amount of corn, a quarter of potatoes, and a modest portion of squash found a place in our fields that season. Uncertainty gnawed at our hearts, unsure if the dam would be completed in time to summon the vitalizing waters. However, as fortune would have it, the dam reached completion in early June. Just in the nick of time, the life-giving waters cascaded into the canal, rescuing our crops from peril and bestowing upon us a modestly fruitful harvest. Our wheat yielded a satisfying fifteen to twenty bushels per acre. With scythes and cradles in hand, we gathered the fruits of our labor, satisfied with the fruits bestowed upon us that summer. Fencing our land occupied a part of our time, for the community shared the responsibility, each member contributing their fair share.

It was the autumn of 1869 when my father, accompanying the first immigrants to journey on the Eastward railroad, arrived in Utah. To meet him, my mother and brother John embarked on a journey with a pair of oxen, traversing the distance to Ogden, the closest point the railroad extended to at that time. Subsequently, upon his arrival in Payson, my father embarked on a pilgrimage to Salt Lake City, to seek an audience with Brigham Young and render his tithes. In the same sacred moments, both he and my mother sought solace within the halls of the Endowment House, their union sealed for eternity.

 Father graced us with his presence that winter, bringing joy to our humble abode. Yet, the untamed nature of the land failed to captivate his spirit. Thus, the following spring witnessed his departure, as he boarded a train bound for New York, setting sail for England. There he resided with my brother George, who had ventured into business on London's Whitechapel Road, where London's "Jack The Ripper" killed his victim's in 1888. So you see, danger can be found anywhere.

Around this juncture, I joined one of Payson's four wards, becoming an ardent member of the church. Meetings and Sunday School became my cherished domains, nurturing my soul. John B. Fairbanks held the mantle of bishop over the four wards, while William Whitehead presided as the elder of the ward to which I pledged my allegiance.

Every week, a convocation of the Elders Quorum bestowed upon me the honor of participation. The weight of the priesthood I carried pressed upon my consciousness, fostering a deeper connection to my faith. I was but eighteen years of age when entrusted with the role of a teacher within our ward.

The verdant canyon enticed the youth to embark on pleasant strolls. In lieu of indulging in ice cream parlors, candy shops, or taverns, we delighted in unearthing the bulbs of the Sego lily, a sweet and refreshing treat. Squaw berries, diminutive fruits no larger than apple seeds, also found favor in our gatherings. Among the favored pastimes of young men and women was a game known as "Copenhagen." In its resemblance to the later "Post office," this game provided an opportunity for acquaintanceship to flourish with the fairer sex.

Samuel's First Wife:

It was during this period that a particular young lady captured my attention. Sarah Eleanor Sabin "Ella", her name sweet upon my tongue, and I embarked on a courtship that spanned several months. Our chosen pastime involved gathering a jovial assembly of kindred spirits, harnessing an ox team, and venturing to Utah Lake for the pursuit of pristine delights. With each passing month, Sarah Eleanor graced my presence more frequently. Choir practice and church meetings became cherished occasions when I could relish her company.

After months of courtship, I summoned the courage to propose matrimony to my beloved. Her heart, too, responded in kind, and she consented to be my cherished wife. The next crucial step required the benevolent blessing of her parents. Hence, one Sunday, as Ella and I sauntered leisurely, I proposed that the time had come to beseech her father and mother for their consent. "Ella," I implored, "I beseech thee to accompany me, that your presence may embolden my spirit." Alas, her response dissipated my hopes, as she demurred, preferring not to join me. I had naught but my own courage to rely upon. Mustering my strength, I knocked upon their door, and her mother, with welcoming tones, beckoned me inside. She inquired about Ella, suspecting my intent. "Yes, indeed," I replied, "I had the pleasure of her company." The lump in my throat swelled, but I persevered. Her father, a man of few words, sat in silence. Moments trickled by before I mustered the strength to utter, "Brother Sabin, I have come to inquire if you harbor any objections to my union with your daughter."

He hesitated, his eyes searching for reassurance that I could provide for her. I assured him, "I shall toil ceaselessly to forge a livelihood for her." His gaze shifted, and he uttered, "Inquire of her mother." And so, I embarked on the arduous task once more. Mrs. Sabin regarded me intently and declared, "If Ella is willing to take that chance, I shall grant my consent." A surge of relief washed over me, dissolving the lump that had plagued my throat. I stepped outside into the garden, where my beloved awaited, and with joyous words, I shared the good tidings.

Then came the time for us to forge our plans, marking the date and hour when we would unite in matrimony, an occasion set for April in the year 1870. In honor of our union, her mother graciously prepared a delightful wedding feast, inviting only a select few dear friends. Since her father was occupied with mining endeavors and spent scarce moments at home, her mother kindly proposed that we reside with them for a spell.

We accepted this generous invitation, yet I swiftly set about constructing a log abode on a plot I had procured beforehand. After three months of wedded bliss, we embarked upon our own dwelling. Contentment and joy filled our hearts. Our humble abode consisted of a single room, measuring fourteen by sixteen feet, with a loft intended for storage. Furnishings were modest: a sturdy stove, a table, a bedstead, two or three chairs, and a couple of benches. Ella possessed her own bedding, and we felt genuinely blessed with our humble provisions.

As winter's icy fingers stretched across the land, we found ourselves in a state of waiting, like a farmer watching the sky for the first signs of rain. The chill settled into our bones, and we longed for the touch of spring's gentle hand upon the earth. Yet, amidst this cold and uncertainty, a visitor was promised, a visitor who would bring warmth to our hearts as surely as the sun unfurls its rays.

In those winter months, my beloved wife sought solace in the embrace of her mother's home, seeking comfort in the company of family. Meanwhile, my path led me to North Tintic, a journey to fashion charcoal for the Salt Lake smelters. Alongside me journeyed my wife's brother, Parley, a sturdy companion in the face of adversity.

But alas, as the winter winds howled their lament, Parley's health began to falter, a flame flickering in the cold. We sold our hard-won charcoal and yet, fate seemed determined to test us further. Parley's strength waned, his spirit dimming like a candle in a gusty night. In the face of his illness, I took upon myself the burden of both teams, both wagons, and pressed onward, determined to deliver Parley safely home.

And when I returned to our humble abode, life had bestowed upon us a radiant gift. A daughter, like a blossom emerging from the snow, had joined our fold. Eight pounds of life, a promise of tomorrow. In honor of my dear mother, we named her, a name that would grace our lips and our hearts—Amy. On the 5th day of February, in the year 1871, she entered this world, her cries like a new song echoing through our log dwelling.

Yet, even in the midst of this joy, a cloud hung heavy over us. Parley, my wife's brother, struggled beneath the weight of his ailment. The coal camp was abandoned, and the approaching spring beckoned us to return to the soil. And so, we left behind the smoky echoes of our charcoal endeavors and turned our hands to the land, to the promise of fresh growth.

In Lavan, my brother Joe had paved his own path, leaving me with the gift of his land. Five acres, a humble expanse, became my canvas for sustenance. As the days lengthened and the earth stirred from slumber, I embarked on a new endeavor, a contract to carve a mile-long ditch for the Payson Cooperative Cattle Company. The sweat of my brow, the strength of my back, they became the tools of progress.

And so, my friends, in this tale, you find the ebb and flow of life, like the seasons that paint the world in hues of change. In the winters of waiting, in the journeys of companionship, and in the new life that springs forth, may you discover the threads that bind us all—our hopes, our dreams, and the unyielding spirit that carries us through it all.

The winds of time carry my memory back to the spring of 1872 a juncture in the tapestry of life when change whispered through the valley like the rustle of leaves in the wind. The Union Pacific, a behemoth of iron and steam, began to lay its tracks through our beloved realm, a venture that promised a bit of labor for willing hands. I, too, found myself entangled in this enterprise, seizing moments between farm furrows to lend my strength to this new creation.

During this time, my oxen, loyal companions of toil, made way for horses, creatures swifter and more versatile. The fields embraced the seed with a renewed vigor, and our journeys became swifter, as the hooves of these noble steeds carried us across the land with newfound ease.

As the sun warmed the earth in the spring of 1872, I felt the urge to expand my domain, to stretch my roots deeper into the soil. An additional five acres became mine, a gift from the land itself, and among my fellow men, a sense of prosperity bloomed. But the year held more for me, as my venturesome spirit led me into the heart of the earth, to the Tintic District, in search of treasures hidden beneath stone and soil. Yet, my miner's dreams yielded meager rewards, and I discovered that the life of a farmer held more allure than that of a miner.

With a handful of cows as companions, their patient eyes watching over the fields, my wife and I toiled together. Butter and milk found eager buyers, and our coffers grew, albeit modestly. The fruits of our labor began to shape our lives, weaving comfort into our modest home.

And then, as autumn leaves danced in the breeze, an opportunity emerged like a hidden gem in the soil. An adobe house, more spacious and promising, beckoned to us, offering three rooms, a pantry, and even a cellar—a place to store the bounty of our harvest and the dreams we nurtured. Our log house, where we had carved our first memories, bid us farewell as we embraced this new abode.

Beside our doorstep, a well was dug, a portal to the life-giving waters that lay beneath. Once, we had fetched water from the nearby creek, a stream that whispered secrets to the wind. Now, our journey to quench our thirst was shortened, as we drew water from the well with buckets, the rhythm of life reflected in its rise and fall.

And so, my friends, these were the seasons of change and growth, of tracks laid and homes built, of journeys taken and dreams pursued. As I look back upon those years, I see them as threads woven into the fabric of a life—a life fashioned from sweat and love, from earth and sky, a life that blossomed amidst the challenges and blessings of time.

Having never received formal education since my youth in Africa, I eagerly embraced the chance to attend night school, seizing the opportunity to expand my knowledge during the winter season. It was around this time that I was appointed to teach a class in Sunday School, an experience that broadened my perspectives on matters of faith. I became deeply engrossed in religious matters, finding profound interest in Bible study.

Indeed, it was the teachings and guidance imparted in Sunday School that safeguarded me from venturing down forbidden paths.

Our second child, Samuel, entered the world in 1873. Following his birth, my wife and I deemed it necessary to journey to the House of the Lord in Salt Lake City, where we could be sealed together by divine authority for time and all eternity, our beloved children united with us. In the fall of 1873, I harnessed my team of horses to our wagon, making preparations for the voyage to Salt Lake. With our equine companions, we completed the journey in two days. Accompanying us were my wife's sister and her husband, John Staheli, who embarked on the same sacred mission.

After arriving in Salt Lake City and resting for the night at a friend's abode, the ensuing day was dedicated to the ordinances performed in the Endowment House. As we commenced our return journey, a tempestuous rainstorm forced us to remain for another day.

Gather 'round, kindred spirits, as we journey back through time to a period of growth and change, when the soil of the earth and the sweat of honest toil intermingled, giving rise to prosperity and trials alike.

As the days of 1874 unfolded, a whisper of transformation danced upon the winds. Up until that juncture, our farming pursuits had been a symphony of sweat and manual labor, where scythes sung their song through the fields and plows carved their stories into the earth. But lo and behold, with the spring's embrace, a new chapter beckoned. I acquired my first reaper and mowing machine—a partnership with the modern that promised to ease the toil of tilling.

And as the blossoms of change opened, so did the embrace of a new crop—alfalfa. Its verdant leaves kissed the earth with promise, offering not only sustenance for our livestock but a bounty of blessings. A venture that began with a patch of land yielded riches of fertilization and profit. With the cutting of the first alfalfa crop, we sowed the seeds of prosperity, letting the second cut go to seed, reaping nature's gifts in the form of eight to ten hundred pounds per acre. And in the market square, these treasures fetched fifteen to twenty cents per pound, a testament to the rewards of patient labor.

The year 1875 carried both joy and sorrow upon its shoulders. As the sun painted the landscape with the hues of life, we acquired an additional ten acres of land, an extension of our domain that spoke of growth and promise. But life's tapestry is woven with both light and shadow, and in the midst of our triumphs, we were struck by loss. Our young son, Samuel Jr., left this world, his journey cut short by the cruel hand of Scarlet Fever. Yet, amidst the tears of farewell, a new chapter unfolded. Our daughter Estella entered the world, a beacon of hope and a reminder that life's circle ever turns.

Within the boundaries of my fields, I nurtured sugar cane, a sweet promise that turned into a flourishing endeavor. In the heart of our region, sugar was a rarity, a luxury whispered about like a secret. And so, my friends, I turned my hands to crafting molasses, a liquid gold that fetched a dollar for every gallon. The market hungered for its sweetness, ensuring my path to prosperity was well-tended.

And then, as the curtain of time unfurled, I joined hands with the United Order—a community built on shared labor and shared bounty. It was a grand venture, where hands and hearts worked as one, and the spoils of our combined efforts were laid bare for all to share. But even in the best of intentions, discord can take root, and alas, the United Order's flame dimmed, a vision that shimmered and then was no more.

So there you have it, a tale of plows and reapers, of alfalfa's green embrace, of molasses's golden allure, and of a communal dream that flickered like a candle's flame. It's a chapter of our history, painted with the hues of sweat, laughter, tears, and the ceaseless rhythm of life.

In the year 1878, our fourth child, David, was born into the world.

As the railroad had only reached as far as Nephi, there existed a great need for teamsters and wagons to facilitate freighting duties. I engaged in this enterprise, hauling various goods such as groceries, dry goods, gunpowder, and even liquor.

Samuel's Second Wife:

Nine years had passed since my marriage to Eleanor, and four children graced our lives when I encountered Emma Erlandson. Celestial marriage, one of the sacred tenets taught by our church, beckoned to me as a devout adherent. Driven by my religious fervor, I yearned to embrace the blessings of the new and everlasting covenant. Upon meeting Emma and becoming acquainted with her, a deep and passionate love kindled within my heart. She possessed a radiant beauty and irresistible charm, and I resolved to make her my wife.

During this period, our church faced uncertainty regarding the government's stance on plural marriage. Consequently, I turned to prayer, seeking divine guidance and an assurance that my path was righteous. When confirmation arrived, assuring me that my supplications were heard, I asked Emma to join me in matrimony. The time and place of that profound moment shall forever remain etched in my memory!

It was mutually agreed upon with my first wife that I embark on this new chapter, for she shared my belief in this sacred principle and wholeheartedly consented to my taking a second wife.

Undeterred by the rumors that pervaded our community, Emma and I resolved to unite in marriage. Together, we journeyed to Salt Lake City, where the sacred ceremony took place on February 27, 1879, in the venerable halls of the Endowment House. Our expedition to Salt Lake City was undertaken by wagon. At daybreak, we loaded our bedding, provisions, and necessary attire into the wagon. Emma, her father Elias Erlandson, and I set forth.

Well, gather 'round once more, dear listeners, for I shall take you on a journey with my first wife, Ella, and my soon to be my second wife, Emma, through the sunlit trails of memory, where adventure and the warmth of the sun painted the canvas of our lives.

Ah, the roads of yester-years, they stretched out like a tale waiting to be told, dusty ribbons under the embrace of the sun's golden touch. The air was filled with the scent of freedom, and the promise of new horizons beckoned. It was a journey that began with excitement, each step echoing with the rhythm of life.

As we set forth, the Provo River whispered its melodies to us, and we rested our weary bones along its banks, sharing sustenance and stories beneath the vast sky. The sun danced on the water, a reflection of the warmth that filled our hearts. With renewed strength, we embarked on the ascent of Provo Bench, a rugged expanse that stretched on for miles, rocky and arid, with naught but the heavens as its canopy. But oh, the beauty of the untamed land, a canvas painted by the hands of nature herself.

And as the evening's embrace drew near, we found ourselves near the point of the mountain, where our campfire's dance painted shadows on the canvas of the night. Supper was a feast for our souls, and as the stars emerged, we found solace beneath their twinkling gaze. Emma and Ella, seeking shelter in the wagon's embrace, and Father Erlandson and I, finding comfort beneath the wagon's sturdy frame, reveled in the stories whispered by the wind.

As the first light of dawn kissed the earth, we rose to greet a new day. Breakfast was shared, horses were harnessed, and the journey resumed. Before the sun had even claimed its throne, Salt Lake City embraced us in its arms. We directed our steps toward a tithing yard, a familiar spot for those on the road.

But the heart of my journey awaited within the walls of the Gardo House, where the President of the Church, John Taylor, resided. His signature was the key, unlocking the door to my heart's desire—the blessing to take a second wife. With grace and kindness, he bestowed his endorsement, a treasure that set my heart aglow.

And so, with the signature of the President and the light of the sun as our guide, Emma and I ventured into the heart of Salt Lake City. Each step was a note in the melody of our journey, a journey where the sunlit trails led not just to a city, but to the tapestry of life itself.

It was Emma's inaugural visit to this metropolis, and her spirit soared with delight as she beheld the city's splendor and marvels. Mules dutifully pulled the streetcars along, while the gas lamps illuminated the thoroughfares. But as the strain of walking took its toll on Emma, we returned to our camp to rest for the coming morrow. With the dawning of the morning, we readied ourselves for the grand occasion, hastening to enter the gates of Temple Square. The Temple, still under construction, had reached the height of its first-story window. Many skilled stone cutters toiled industriously, fashioning a bustling scene.

We proceeded into the Endowment House to partake in sacred rituals. We disclosed our ages and the names of our fathers and mothers. Then we stood prepared for the sacred bond of matrimony, uniting us for time and all eternity.

Once the ceremony concluded, the day still young, we engaged in some shopping and made arrangements to return home. On our first night's journey, we reached the precipice of the mountain and halted there to camp. Blessed with a fleet-footed team, we made good progress, arriving home early the following day. Emma's mother had lovingly prepared a bountiful family supper for our arrival, as Ella and the children were also present.

The weather bestowed its benevolence, enabling me to promptly prepare my land for sowing. By the end of February, the majority of my grain had been sown. However, the first day of March unleashed a fearsome snowstorm, inflicting significant damage upon the trees. Subsequently, a frigid winter took hold, its icy grip unforgiving.
The ensuing summer was dedicated to embellishing my abode, reuniting my entire family, and tending to my land. As autumn approached, my efforts focused on toiling in the canyon, securing the winter's wood, our sole source of fuel. Furthermore, plowing commenced in preparation for the coming year, and the corn required shucking and shelling, serving as sustenance for our livestock and a means of trade. In those early times, the opportunities for converting one's toil into monetary gain were meager.

In the spring of 1880, I erected a new log cabin on the farm, a mere two-mile distance from our previous dwelling. I delved into the earth, excavating a well, and constructed enclosures. Then, I relocated Emma to this newfound haven.

That spring arrived tardily, its delay attributed to a harsh winter. Consequently, my efforts

Brigham Young University Lee Library L. Tom Perry Special Collections; MSS P 1

to sow wheat were similarly delayed. Nevertheless, nature bestowed upon us an abundant harvest that season.

Persecution of the Polygamists begins:

Emma had scarcely spent two or three months in her new sanctuary when the winds of persecution grew fiercer. The government commenced arresting brethren who maintained plural families, compelling us to send Emma away for a brief respite. She sought solace in Ogden Valley, dwelling amongst dear friends. It was during her sojourn there that her son George entered this world on the 11th of November, 1880.

Meanwhile, I undertook renovations upon our ancestral home, adding two rooms, a pantry, and a basement. As was customary, I diligently harvested, secured our stockpile of firewood, and made general provisions for the impending winter.

A few days preceding Christmas, Emma returned to our abode, cradling our infant son. The joy that welled within us at her homecoming was immeasurable.

Now, for I've got story, a tale of trials and steadfast hearts amidst a storm of persecution that raged not only in the skies but within the halls of power.

You see, as the winter winds howled, another kind of storm brewed far from the snowy landscapes. It was in those distant chambers of Congress that laws were born, laws aimed to quell a way of life dear to the hearts of many. The air was heavy with tension, and the hearts of the Saints were cast in shadows.

Then came the Edmonds Tucker, anti-polygamy law, its words etched in ink but carrying a weight far heavier than any parchment. And as it settled like a dark cloud over the land, the forces of those who deemed themselves righteous bearers of the law grew bolder, their eyes gleaming with zealous determination. They prowled the streets and corners, eyes sharp and ears eager to catch whispers of polygamist families and where they lived.

In the midst of this turmoil, amid the storm that threatened to uproot the very essence of my faith, but I remained unwavering. I, with my heart tethered to the land I tended, my horse saddled and ready as a steadfast companion, found my strength in the rhythm of life I and my wives, Ella and Emma had built.

Farming became not just a means of sustenance, but a testament to resilience. Livestock were not just creatures, but symbols of a way of life that had stood the test of time. And within the walls of the church, my steps remained resolute, ecclesiastical duties shouldered with the weight of devotion.

But it was not just the toil of the fields that sustained us. No, it was the prayers that echoed in the corners of my home, like whispers of hope in the darkest of nights. It was the tithes dutifully paid, not as mere coins but as symbols of unwavering commitment. And in the midst of adversity, church obligations were not burdens, but beacons that guided us through the storm.

So, my friends, in the face of laws and forces that sought to bend our spirits, we stood strong. We held onto our faith, not just as a belief, but as a shield. And as the world outside churned with chaos, our hearts remained a steady anchor, tethered to the rhythms of life and faith that had carried our people through the ages.

Moving Second Wife to a Secure Location:

Emma continued to dwell in our ancestral abode until she bore four children: George, Elias, Joseph, and Sarah. However, the intensity of persecution reached such heights that I ultimately found myself compelled to relocate Emma and our entire brood to the South.

In October of 1897, we packed our provisions and embarked on our journey. Destinations were uncertain, but we set our course toward the South. On our inaugural night, we rested in Levan. My brother Joseph resided there and advised me to consider Escalante. The following day, our caravan reached Gunnison, where benevolent strangers offered us lodgings for the night. The coldness of the evening made their kindness all the more cherished. At first light, we settled our debts and resumed our journey, advancing to Salina for a midday repast. There, we were informed of an eastern shortcut, sparing us the need to ford the Sevier River. Alas, our progress through a meadow proved treacherous, as the soft ground ensnared our wheels, requiring assistance before we could extricate ourselves.

A farmhouse stood nearby, our beacon of hope for aid. Regrettably, our pleas were met with refusal. However, fortune favored us when we encountered a man engaged in the arduous task of "Pole Tax." Upon beseeching him for the use of his team, he readily acquiesced, lending a hand in our liberation from the mire. A farmer residing at the mouth of Clear Creek Canyon, he extended an invitation for us to spend the night. We passed a delightful evening in his company, and he urged us to venture through Clear Creek Canyon, opining that the road offered superior passage compared to King's Meadow.

Taking his counsel to heart, we embarked upon the chosen path, a journey fraught with challenges as we traversed hills and valleys, groves of pinion pine and cedar. The untamed landscape unfolded before us in wild, fantastical splendor. Around noon, we crossed paths with three men traveling in a wagon. Their presence brought solace, as they guided us toward the road that would lead us into Grass Valley.

In our conversation, I gleaned that these men, too, sought refuge from the watchful eyes of the law. The day was well-advanced when we arrived at the head of Grass Valley. Though wearied, the road ahead proved more favorable, and we journeyed along the valley's eastern side, eventually reaching a ranch house. The proprietor, a prosperous rancher, graciously received us. His domain boasted a spacious house and barn, and the meadow abounded with cattle.

We sought permission to camp for the night, to which he assented, welcoming us into his abode, warmed by a crackling fire. A bachelor of refined education, he explained that he sought respite in these surroundings for the betterment of his health. Our conversation with him inspired a change of heart within me—I resolved to redirect our path toward Rabbit Valley instead of Escalante.

That morning, we bid our gracious host farewell and embarked upon our journey across the rugged Fish Lake Mountains toward Rabbit Valley. The arduous ascent was made difficult by treacherous roads, marked with ditches, hills, and valleys. At long last, we reached the pinnacle of a hill where we paused to partake of a well-deserved lunch. From this vantage point, we gazed upon the inviting valley spread out below. Eagerly, we commenced our descent, encountering steep sections of road and traversing lengthy slopes before reaching the valley floor. The day was nearly spent by the time we descended into the valley. As we neared the settlement of Loa, providence crossed our path in the form of a mounted man. Unfamiliar with the locality, we halted him to seek guidance. Kindly, he welcomed us to his abode in Fremont. Accepting his invitation, we embarked together, our new acquaintance sharing our company and disclosing their need for a schoolteacher. Should I possess the requisite skills, gainful employment awaited me.

60

The sun had long since dipped below the horizon as we arrived at his humble dwelling. His wife greeted us warmly, and we whiled away the evening engaged in conversation about the local terrain. Inquiring about the whereabouts of Franklin Young, I discovered that he resided in Teasdale, some eighteen miles distant. As Franklin Young was my brother-in-law, I resolved to journey to that pleasant hamlet. Grateful for the kindness shown by our newfound friends, we expressed our heartfelt appreciation and embarked toward Teasdale, traversing the length of the idyllic valley.

Nightfall found us halting at Thurber, for the inclement weather had impeded our progress. Seeking respite, we were received by a young couple, the Forsythes, who had recently completed their own abode. Supper graced our weary souls with its bounty, featuring the richness of cold milk and freshly baked salt-rising bread—a delicacy we had not enjoyed since our departure from Payson. The next day, having settled our lodging accounts, we resumed our journey toward Teasdale, a mere five miles distant.

The arrival of our kith and kin was met with surprise and delight, and our hearts swelled with joy at the sight of loved ones. They opened their arms and home to us, extending a warm welcome. After a few days spent acquainting ourselves with the surroundings, I made the decision to make Teasdale our permanent abode.

Once Emma and the children had settled in, I made my return to Payson, where my responsibilities awaited. Bees required tending, hogs needed slaughtering, cows awaited milking, and the cattle mustered for the approaching winter. With my children still in their tender years, the labor fell squarely upon my shoulders, for Ella was occupied with the care of our own brood. Five little ones now graced our family, with the arrival of David, joining William, Frankie, and Emma, although Frankie's time among us was tragically fleeting, much like our son Samuel.

My days were consumed with ecclesiastical duties, attending to my church obligations, teaching and ministering to the ailing. However, the time had come to make arrangements for the journey to Teasdale, laden with provisions and furniture, as well as the acquisition of a horse. The return trip lacked eventfulness, as familiarity with the

Brigham Young University Lee Library L. Tom Perry Special Collections, MSS P 1

route guided me, and I traversed the path alone, seeking refuge in my wagon each night. Though the divide presented me with considerable snow, I arrived in Teasdale on the auspicious day of February 14, 1888.

Upon my arrival, Emma had diligently prepared our new dwelling, and our furniture found its place within its walls. Once settled, we relished the comfort and happiness that emanated from this, Emma's first true home. It was my intention to remain by her side throughout the year. The bishop swiftly welcomed us into the ward, where we found purpose and contentment. We discharged our duties with diligence and reveled in the embrace of the community.

Persecution Grows More Bitter:

In January of the following year, Bishop Taylor of Fremont arrived, accompanied only by his plural wife, seeking refuge from pursuing deputies. Bound for Old Mexico, he invited me to accompany him, hoping that I too might find a place in that land. The January chill gripped us as we embarked on our journey, heading southward through the Junction, where one branch led to Blue Valley and the other to Hall's Crossing Road. There, we chanced upon an abandoned path, once traversed by intrepid pioneers who sought settlement in San Juan County. Barely more than a trail, it proved challenging to navigate. At one point, we inadvertently strayed onto a cattle trail, losing our way entirely.

Faced with uncertainty, deprived of sustenance and water, I turned to the Lord, beseeching divine guidance. Kneeling humbly, facing the east atop a small ridge, I fervently sought the Lord's intervention. I implored Him to illuminate the path before us, to pardon our deficiencies, and to deliver us from our adversaries. With closed eyes, I awaited a response, and suddenly, a vision unfolded before me. I beheld a man astride a white mule, journeying southward, with the understanding that he would guide us. Grateful for the assurance that my prayer would be answered, I rose from my supplication.

Upon my return to camp, Brother Taylor inquired about my findings. Eagerly, I beckoned him to accompany me, assuring him that we would discover both water and assistance along our path. As we descended the slope, I recounted my vision to him, when lo and behold, a man riding a white creature materialized in the distance, moving toward the south. Catching sight of us, he halted momentarily, undoubtedly puzzled by the presence of a covered wagon. He then approached us, and we converged near the creek while our horses quenched their thirst. Inquisitive, he asked, "Where are you headed?"

Upon learning of our quest to find Hall's Crossing, he informed me that it lay several miles to the south. He also revealed that he found himself in those parts due to a necessary visit to a nearby mine for tire repairs. The discovery of his presence filled us with elation, and he kindly offered his aid in locating Hall's Crossing. While he and Brother Taylor forged ahead on horseback to scout the trail, I followed, guiding the two teams of horses to the best of my ability, traversing hills, hollows, and the meandering creek. Eventually, our collective efforts bore fruit as we arrived at Hall's Crossing, a small assemblage of placer miners panning for gold. When they diligently toiled, these miners earned modest sums of $2.50 to $5.00 per day.

Listen closely, my friends, for this part of my story holds the weight of trials unforeseen, challenges towering like mountains before a weary traveler. As we made our way downward, the river's edge beckoned, but it was no simple path. With every step, we took caution, for the edge was a precipice, and our wagons, laden with our hopes and dreams, could easily tumble into the churning, frothy waters of the mighty Colorado River.

Oh, the river! Its name carried the weight of legends, and as we gazed upon its surging waters, we knew a new challenge awaited. There was no ferry here, no easy crossing. The river, untamed and wild, roared with fierce rapids, a torrent of white water cascading downstream. But we were not ones to be daunted by nature's fury.

Fortune smiled upon us, for a flat boat, worn and weathered, lay waiting beyond the rapids. It had been the lifeline of miners, a bridge across the roaring waters. We enlisted a miner's help, and with sturdy ropes, we tied ourselves to the boat, determined to tame the river's rage. Two souls, one boat, against the rushing current, the icy waters gnashing at our courage.

Oh, it was a bitter day, the cold slicing through our garments like a knife. The ground beneath our feet was a treacherous dance of slush and ice. But there was a wagon on the other side, waiting to be unloaded and carried across. And so, with the miner in the boat, I braced myself against the current, hauling the vessel upstream, my muscles straining against the river's wrath.

Brother Taylor, patient and unwavering, stood on the other side, ready to dismantle the wagon and prepare it for its watery voyage. The day stretched long, the sun sinking behind the mountains, and still, I persisted. My body was soaked, frozen, and my belly empty, yet my spirit burned like a flame.

Desperation drove me to a nearby camp of miners. I offered them a handsome sum for their aid, a sum that would make a man's eyes widen. But one among them, bold and unyielding, refused with a grin, declaring not even $20.00 a day would tempt him. I returned to my labor, my frozen clothes clinging to me, my limbs aching.

And then, my friends, with the help of one courageous miner, victory! The boat reached its destination, and the wagon, patiently waiting, was soon on the move again. The river, tamed by our resolve, carried us onward, its roar echoing in our ears. And as I sat by the fire that night, warmth seeping back into my body, I couldn't help but feel a sense of triumph, for the river had challenged us, but we had conquered.

With the river's challenge still fresh in our minds. The setting sun cast long shadows as our preparations for loading the boats began. Three trips it would take, back and forth across the river, a dance with the waters.

The hours slipped by, weariness tugging at us like a heavy cloak. The miner, his heart touched by our persistence, hesitantly agreed to stay and help us complete the task. His eyes held the weariness of many journeys, his hands roughened by the trials of the land. We paid him what he asked, a fair price for his sweat and toil.

Our wagons were ready, but our horses, noble companions of our journey, still awaited their turn. A long rope was fastened to one, and with Taylor and his wife aboard the small boat, they set out, leading the horse across the river's current. I stayed on the shore, guiding the rest of the horses, their hooves splashing in the icy waters. The river, a relentless beast, challenged us at every step.

One by one, they crossed, and as the last hoof found firm ground, Taylor returned for me. The darkness surrounded us, a shroud of uncertainty, but the fire we built held back the shadows. Our clothes, wet from the river's embrace, found warmth and solace by the crackling flames. Supper was a simple affair, nourishment for bodies weary from the day's struggle. Our faithful horses, they too were cared for, tethered close and fed grain to sustain them through the night.

The morning sun found us at our tasks again, the river's chill still in the air. Our horses, set free to graze, their heads bent low to the earth, finding sustenance in the land. And we, we toiled through the night, reuniting wagons and loading them with our hopes and dreams.

But the day's challenges were far from over. As the sun climbed higher, voices carried across the river, voices loud and demanding. Two figures emerged from the opposite side, deputies in search of those who dared to live contrary to the law. They had lost their way, stumbling upon our camp. Their demands were clear—turn back, they commanded.

Yet we, my friends, we stood firm. Refusing their orders, we urged them to stay put. A gunshot echoed through the canyon, a sound meant to be a warning, to show them that we would not be cowed. And as the echoes faded, the wilderness around us held its breath. No more shouts, no more threats. We held our ground, ready to face whatever challenges the world might throw our way.

Ah, the journey through those towering mountains continues, with Taylor leading us like a beacon through the rugged unknown. The cliffs rose above, the jagged teeth of the land's embrace. A path, hidden in the folds of this rocky expanse, was our only guide. Oh, how we unloaded and reloaded those wagons, each step a victory against the landscape's obstinacy. It felt like the earth itself resisted our passage, clinging to our wheels.

The path, if one could call it that, was but a memory of those who had come before us—a mere whisper in the rocks, the occasional tire marks guiding our way. The land, like an ancient giant, rolled beneath our wheels, its shoulders sloping toward the distant horizon. Water, the nectar of life, became a dire need. Our supplies dwindled like whispers carried by the wind.

Taylor, brave as a mountain lion, rode ahead, searching for signs, while I maneuvered the wagon as best I could, tracing the tire marks etched on the rugged canvas of the land. A small hill revealed a hidden gem—a hollowed rock holding rainwater like a precious jewel. Bugs and scum were cleared away, and its cool liquid offered solace to our parched throats. With our cans filled and the horses tethered, we paused in this hidden oasis, our spirits renewed by the gift of water.

Night descended, and with it came the haunting cry of coyotes. Our camp, a flicker of life amidst this desolation, was hushed by the chilling wind. Our horses, our companions on this odyssey, grazed on the patch of grass that dared to thrive here. The stars above, a tapestry of distant dreams, witnessed our solitude.

65

The dawn unfurled, a canvas painted with the same hues of struggle and determination. Every day mirrored the last—endless travel, the search for water's hidden pockets, the forge of our path through the unyielding wilderness. The rhythm of our days was the rhythm of nature, slow and deliberate, punctuated by the distant cries of coyotes, as if they were the guardians of this untamed land.

And so, my friends, the road stretched before us, unyielding and unforgiving, yet our spirits remained unbroken. We carried with us the memory of water's relief, the solace of campfires in the midst of desolation, and the company of horses who, like us, pressed on. The journey was not easy, but it was our path, and we trod it with courage, finding strength in the face of adversity.

My memory takes us to late January, when the San Juan River welcomed us to its rocky embrace down in New Mexico. Our wagon wheels stirred the earth, and our hearts were filled with a blend of curiosity and caution. Our first encounter along this river's course was a trading post owned by Navaho Indians. A wooden haven nestled amidst the wild, it beckoned with promises of sustenance.

I stepped into that humble establishment, a structure that held secrets of the land within its wooden walls. Men conversed in a corner, their faces bearing stories etched by life's trials. Amidst them stood a woman, a rare sight in such environs. "Do you have any provisions to spare?" I asked, my voice mingling with the whispers of the place. They motioned me toward the rear, assuring me of abundance. Skepticism lingered in my mind, but curiosity spurred me on.

Behind the curtains of the trading post, a man emerged. His hand extended, bearing a piece of meat as a gift from this realm. Gratitude painted my voice as I thanked him, returning to our wagon with a sense of awe. The journey pressed on, like the river's steady current, until we found ourselves in Bluff City as the sun's last light painted the sky.

Bluff City, nestled amid those towering red bluffs, welcomed us with open arms. A Mormon settlement, it exuded warmth, a stark contrast to the wild landscapes that surrounded it. For two days, we rested our weary bones, taking refuge in this pocket of civilization. Letters were penned, tales shared, and the rustling leaves of life's pages were momentarily stilled.

In the hushed corners of Bluff City, we learned the truth behind that trading post. A hushed whisper revealed a tale of murder, etched in blood on this very land. The locals shared secrets, revealing the post's darker history, where trading was tainted with tragedy. Card games and exchanges, mingling with danger. Shooting incidents, a canvas painted with violence.

Under the moon's gaze, trouble stirred the air. As night's embrace wrapped around us, I lay in my bed, the creaks of the earth's floorboards composing a lullaby. Footsteps approached, whispers of moccasins against the ground. An Indian figure emerged from the shadows, his eyes meeting mine, and then he fled, vanishing like a ghost of the night. Trouble and tension lingered, woven into the tapestry of these lands.

With dawn's light, we resumed our journey along the San Juan River's winding course. The day greeted us with icy winds, a reminder that nature's forces could be as unforgiving as they were awe-inspiring. Along our path, we encountered abandoned ranches, their windows boarded, their stories lost to the wind. It seemed the turmoil with the Indians had forced these homesteaders to leave, their dreams buried beneath the shifting sands of change.

Progress became a battle against nature's whims, the drifting sands swallowing our footsteps, our wagon's wheels fighting against the earth's grip. The San Juan River flowed beside us, a witness to our determination, and the land whispered secrets as ancient as time itself.

That night, we camped on the desert's outskirts, on the boundary line of the newly formed states: Utah, Arizona, New Mexico, and Colorado. The night sky revealed its clarity, while the menacing howls of the coyotes filled the air. Their hunger seemed endless, for the aroma of our frying bacon wafted through the surroundings. With the break of dawn, we continued our journey, traversing valleys and ascending bluffs.

At long last, we arrived at a place called Oleo, later known as Fruita—a charming village built by the Mormons on the banks of the San Juan River. We pitched our camp, acquainting ourselves with some of the locals. Through conversation, we learned that Apostle Young resided there, using the name Dr. Hogan to elude the deputies.

Eager to meet him, we made inquiries, yet no one seemed to know of his presence or had a desire to disclose it, unaware of our identities. Disheartened, we departed a Brother's residence named Stevens, when suddenly a voice called out to us. It was the Apostle himself. He stated, "I observed you boys through the window and had the impression that we might be of assistance to each other. Now, what can I do for you?"

We entered and held a council, though the prospects for continuing our journey appeared unfavorable. Our intended destination lay in Old Mexico, yet Elder Taylor deemed it prudent to remain in Oleo for the season. He selected a spot along the LePlat River, where he planted grain. Meanwhile, I stayed with the Stevens family, who requested my aid with various tasks. I constructed a well for them and threshed one hundred bushels of wheat, as machinery was scarce in those days.

Several families of Saints resided there, and I found joy in attending church and participating in choir practice. The Apostle had a mission for the church, which required his presence in Durango. He enlisted my help, and together we embarked on a route that took us up the San Juan River, passing through Farmington. Departing from there, we journeyed along the Animas River. During our travels, we camped near a dilapidated Indian village called Aztec.

Gather 'round, dear reader, for the story winds deeper into the folds of history, a journey etched by encounters with the unexpected. It was a time when the voice of Apostle Young held wisdom that carved its mark upon hearts.

Picture it: Apostle Young and I, side by side, traversing life's path. As our steps danced to the rhythm of the road, his voice held curiosity, a curiosity that soon unearthed my motivation for venturing into the lands of Mexico. With candor, I laid my cards upon the table, revealing my truth. "It's Mexico or imprisonment," I confessed. His wise eyes met mine, an unspoken understanding passing between us.

With that exchange, his counsel flowed like a river's current. "Mexico may not be your wisest path, my friend," his words, like tendrils of smoke, unfurled. A path of advice laid before me, urging me to consider an alternative. But my worries, like persistent shadows, still danced in my mind. The threat of imprisonment loomed, a storm cloud in an otherwise clear sky.

It was then, in that moment, that Apostle Young's voice became a lifeline. His tone was firm, yet reassuring, his words painting a portrait of hope against the canvas of my fears. "Brother Francom," he said, his voice carrying the weight of promise, "if you return home, tend to your kin, you won't face the prison's cold embrace." Those words, like a warm blanket on a winter's night, wrapped around me. Assurance, a balm to my soul, mending the frayed edges of my spirit. And in that heartbeat, my path was illuminated.

Through that journey, Apostle Young ceased to be just a leader. He became a mentor, a friend, his presence a guiding light. Durango welcomed us, its rugged charm softened by the mountains that cradled it. A frontier town, wild and untamed, revealing its beauty against the backdrop of nature's grandeur. Seeking rest, we took refuge in a local inn, a safe haven for the night's embrace.

There, in the hush of solitude, I turned to my prayers. Secret devotion, hidden from the world's eyes, echoed within those four walls. Apostle Young, a sage in his own right, cautioned against openly baring our faith in this foreign place. The sands of caution whispered their secrets to us, and we heeded their warnings.

Durango, with its rough-hewn edges, was a place where voices reverberated with recklessness, where the heartbeats of temperance fell on deaf ears. Opportunities for work beckoned with alluring wages, yet the silent expectation was that the coin earned would dance away as quickly as it was earned. A town where the ghosts of fleeting pleasures waltzed with the winds.

With the morning sun's first touch, Apostle Young's path diverged from mine. His journey led him to Fort Winegate in Arizona, leaving me alone to face the river's current, relying solely on a humble wagon to bear me forward. The wheels of destiny spun, each rotation carrying me deeper into the realm of uncertainty.

On the second night of my solitary journey, I made camp later than expected. As I busied myself preparing a modest meal, the distant sound of approaching wagons reached my ears. They arrived at the road and halted. One of the men ventured toward my fire, inquiring if I was alone and humbly requesting to camp alongside me. Their party consisted of four wagons, housing two families. They relayed that they had been advised against traveling through that treacherous territory alone due to the natives' overt hostility. These individuals, who were not of our faith, further informed me of a small Mormon settlement down the way, purportedly consorting with the Indians. Determined to stand united, they elected to stay together, and so I bid them farewell come morning.

Subsequently, I sought solace amidst a grove of cottonwood trees, seeking refuge from the forceful gusts that swept across the land. Settling down early for the night, I slipped into slumber, only to be greeted by a vivid dream urging me to relocate my camp. Roused from my sleep, the recollection of President Woodruff's admonition resonated within me, compelling me to act. I harnessed the horses and shifted my camp to the protective bluff. As fortune would have it, the winds raged even fiercer, and when daybreak graced the horizon, I witnessed the spot where I had initially pitched my camp now adorned with fallen trees.

The sun had painted the sky with hues of amber and gold, as I descended along the San Juan River's banks. Each step, a dance of resilience, brought me closer to my destination, a settlement embraced by the land's tender embrace. Yet, as fate would have it, it wasn't the town's streets or its buildings that would seize my attention, but the faces that held stories and secrets of their own - the faces of the Navaho Indians.

Troubles had cast their shadow upon this native tribe, their faces etched with worry and discomfort. Word had danced upon the winds, whispering tales of my knowledge, my healing touch. And so, like a moth drawn to a flame, they approached me, their eyes carrying a silent plea for relief.

One among them, tormented by the agony of a toothache, stepped forward with a request. The air was pregnant with uncertainty, my heart pounding like the distant drums. To extract a tooth, a delicate dance between skill and courage, a dance where the wrong step could lead to pain and failure. For a heartbeat, my hesitation clung to the air, like dew upon morning grass.

Yet, deep within my being, memories stirred - memories of other moments, other teeth, extracted with care and precision. A calm voice, not my own, echoed within me, whispering tales of triumphs long past. The decision was made, and I nodded, a quiet affirmation of his task.

They gathered around, the Navaho and I, a fusion of worlds and hopes. Amidst the whispering leaves and the river's murmurs, I laid the man on the ground, his pain etched upon his face, his trust shimmering in his eyes. Above him, the sky held its breath, the sun casting its tender gaze upon the scene.

A prayer, silent yet fervent, drifted from the my heart. My hands moved with precision, guided by a wisdom that seemed more ancient than time itself. In that sacred moment, a symphony of humanity and nature played out, the man's tooth releasing its grip, like a prisoner set free.

The sighs of relief, a chorus of gratitude, swept through the gathering. Eyes that had held worry now glimmered with newfound hope. The Navaho watched, their hearts etching the wanderer's image into their collective memory, a healer whose touch held the power to transform pain into liberation.

And so, as the sun painted the sky with shades of twilight, I, a mear wanderer in this land, walked away from that encounter, my heart heavy with the weight of a moment's significance. In a world woven with stories, my journey had converged with others', weaving a thread of healing, of shared humanity, of a kindness that transcended boundaries.

Oh, the tales the rivers could tell, the whispers of history carried upon their currents. And this, my friends, was just one chapter, one encounter, one brushstroke on the canvas of time.

Oh my memories, how they fill the tapestry of time, where the flickering lantern lights and the coal dust-filled air spun the fabric of existence. In a realm where life's chapters were written by toil and faith, my story unfolds, one of hardship and healing, of human connection and the divine touch.

Amidst the depths of a coal mine, where the earth's treasures lay in the embrace of darkness, I found myself alongside Mr. Stevens, a fellow seeker of fortune buried beneath layers of coal and sweat. With each swing of the pickaxe, the promise of monetary gain echoed in our ears, a melody carried by the echoing thuds of hard labor. At day's end, I was offered refuge within Mr. Stevens' quarters, a haven from the shadows of the mine.

But life's currents are as unpredictable as a wild river, and on one eve, Mrs. Stevens' voice echoed with urgency, her words summoning me to her son's dwelling where his wife had been in labor for 3 days.. There, in the midst of the woman's pain and her silent cries, he faced the raw vulnerability of birth's ordeal.

The young woman lay upon her bed, her face etched with the marks of struggle, her hands reaching out for solace. I, a mere wandering soul, a vessel of ancient rites, assumed my role, my palms anointed with sacred oil and placed upon this womens head, with my heart heavy with the weight of my priesthood duty. In fervent supplication, I reached out to the heavens, beseeching the divine hands to ease her path.

And as the air held its breath, as if the universe itself paused to witness, a tender cry broke through the room. In the hallowed space, the sacred prayers intertwined with the newborn's first wails, an embrace of life's beginning and the embrace of the eternal.

A touch, gentle yet profound, bridged the realms of humanity and the divine. The woman's hands clung to the wanderer's neck, a gesture that seemed to tether her to life itself, as if the act of grasping held the power to pull her from the abyss of suffering.

In that precious instant, as I knelt, my hands upon her brow and her infant's cries resonating like a chorus of angels, the threads of fate wove a story of hope. The birthing pains receded, replaced by the dawn of new life.

From that moment, the bond between me and the family deepened, threads of gratitude and reverence weaving their stories together. A woman once ensnared by suffering now cradled a child in her arms, a gift born from the echo of prayers and the touch of a stranger who was, in truth, no stranger at all.

In the coal mine's shadow and the heart's recesses, a tale was written—a tale of labor and miracles, of coal dust and sacred oils, of lives interwoven by circumstance and sealed by grace. And as time flowed like a river, carrying stories on its currents, this one, too, found its place, a flickering star within the night sky of remembrance.

In March, the heart of the year's rebirth, when winter's chill loosened its grip and the air seemed to dance with the promise of spring, I found himself once again in the company of Apostle Young. The roads we tread were the same ones he had ventured upon before, yet now, a different light shimmered upon the horizon.

As we journeyed, the Apostle's presence cast a unique aura, and the settlements we visited bustled with excitement, as if their arrival was marked by fate itself. The people gathered, eager to hear his words, to glean wisdom from his lips, and to bask in the warmth of his spiritual guidance. With each stop, new faces and old acquaintances merged into a mosaic of faith and fellowship.

Yet, as the wheels of fate continued their inexorable turn, we found themselves at the familiar threshold of the Colorado River. But this time, the heavens themselves seemed to weep, tears of rain descending from the sky and mingling with the river's ceaseless flow. I, a mere wanderer, grumbled, my voice a companion to the relentless raindrops that drenched the land. But in this very discomfort, Apostle Young found providence, a sign heralding unseen trouble.

Miraculously, the land appeared deserted, a stage upon which only the two men and their appointed boatmen danced their watery pas de deux. Dandy Crossing awaited, a crossing that was anything but dandy in its formidable waters. Yet, two men, perhaps angels in disguise, appeared at this junction, ready to transport them across.

The wagons, loaded with the burdens of the journey, were ushered onto the boat, a floating sanctuary amidst the river's turbulent embrace. Horses, noble companions of the journey, next entered the fray. Apostle Young and Brother Taylor joined them on the vessel, while I remained anchored to the shore, a conductor of equine souls.

Together, we enticed the horses into the water, coaxing them against the river's demanding will. A gray horse, like a spirited apparition, swayed dangerously toward the boat, its presence a potential peril. Sacrificing the reins, the gray was released to the river's care, becoming both a sentinel of the current's strength and a tribute to the force of nature.

In the storm's tumult, one of our party fell ill, the battle against the elements and the river's might sapping his strength. The wagon cover was discarded, a gesture to maintain the delicate balance of their fragile vessel. I stepped up, my oar in hand, determination ignited by duty.

Rowing against the wind's fierce resistance, they propelled the vessel onward, a minnow in the belly of the tempest. The storm's hand pushed them downstream, like pieces on a celestial game board. Yet, in the ebb and flow of adversity, we persevered. The river's tribulation finally subsided, releasing us onto the solid ground of a sandy haven, horses and wagons carried to safety on its back.

And so, in this dance between water and land, between the embrace of nature's fury and the steadfastness of human spirit, we moved forward. The Apostle's presence, a beacon of guidance, and my resilience, a testament to the strength of faith and duty, wove a narrative of trials met and adversity conquered.

Having subsisted on an empty stomach since morning, I sought respite in a sheltered spot shielded from the biting wind, eager to halt our journey for the night. However, the resolute Apostle disregarded my plea, insisting that we ascend to the bluff.

Providentially, we heeded his counsel, for as night befell us, the ravine through which we had previously passed was engulfed in torrents of water.

Continuing our odyssey through Graves Valley, tracing the winding path of the dirty Devil River, Apostle Young divulged his desire for me to accompany him to Teton Valley, assuring me that I would receive a summons when the time was right. However, fate intervened, as Apostle Young was summoned to embark on a mission to England.

Thus, I settled in Teasdale, devoting my efforts to toiling for the Utah Nursery Company. I erected a dwelling for my family, adorning the land with an orchard.
Gathering cattle for the company, I herded them to Salt Lake City. When autumn descended, I escorted my family to Payson, where we spent a blissful six weeks in the company of Emma's mother. It was during this

period that we ventured to the Manti Temple, dedicating our children to our loving care. Ella, along with Emma's parents, returned to Payson, while Emma and I retraced our steps to Teasdale. One fateful night, as we made camp, snow fell relentlessly upon us, and I fell ill. With no other recourse, my nine-year-old son, George, assumed the reins, guiding the horses up a treacherous incline where every step seemed to carry them backward rather than forward.

Come December, I made my return to Payson. Before bidding farewell to the valley, my dear friend Archie Young and I embarked on a quest to procure a deer or two in the majestic Fish Lake Mountains. Equipped with a modest wagon, a team of horses, and provisions, we ventured into a grove of pine trees, guaranteeing ample fuel for our camp. Though the snowfall had intensified, we pressed on, nearing Fish Lake in search of our elusive quarry. At a small clearing, we decided to part ways, each taking a wide circle in hopes of a successful encounter. Yet, as the storm raged with unremitting fervor, enormous snowflakes swirling amidst the howling wind, I discerned the perils of the deteriorating conditions.

Reluctantly, I retreated to camp, the darkness enveloping me, my solitude palpable. Firing my rifle into the gloom, I sought a response, but only the echoes returned my call. Sensing my disorientation, I resolved to ignite a fire, laboring diligently to find dry kindling amidst the unrelenting dampness. Eventually, I succeeded in creating a blaze, positioning myself close for warmth and security. With a stockpile of firewood, I safeguarded myself from the chilling cold. I remained in constant motion, combating the biting frost, my meager coat offering scant protection against the elements, and a profound sense of vulnerability seized me in the desolate night.

I grew weary, so I gathered timber and constructed a makeshift platform to rest upon, with a fire beneath me to ward off the chill. In the dead of night, one of the towering pine trees caught ablaze, eventually collapsing onto the scaffold where I lay. Sleep eluded me thereafter, for fear of further mishaps. With the break of dawn, I readied myself to return to the place where we had left the wagon, uncertain if my companion had returned but hopeful that he had. Setting forth, I found the snow reaching my hips. Guided by the moon's gentle glow, I trudged southward, battling the treacherous terrain, yet I failed to locate our camp. As evening drew near, exhausted and famished, I finally descended into the valley.

There, I stumbled upon a farmhouse and recounted to the lady of the house how I had been lost in the mountains throughout the night. Compassionately, she bestowed food upon me and revealed that my companion had already descended, organizing a search party to find me. Anxious to cease their efforts, I implored her to dispatch her young son on horseback to Freemont, where the search party had convened, to relay the news of my safety. Grateful for her aid, I made my way to Archie Young's nearby abode. He confessed the anguish he had experienced, fearing the somber duty of delivering sorrowful tidings to my kin, yet he rejoiced at being spared such a burden. The following morning, bidding farewell to my friend, I embarked on a journey over the mountains toward Payson. Unremarkable was my passage to that destination, where I found Ella and our family in good health.

I rounded up the few cattle that I possessed in the field and tended to their needs. Engaging in the church's labor, I fulfilled my duties as a teacher, visiting the faithful Saints. Throughout that winter and summer, I remained in Payson, devoted to farming and fortifying my land with sturdy fences. A bountiful harvest of wheat, corn, and potatoes rewarded my toil.

Once the harvest was complete and the hogs were slaughtered, I ventured south to attend to the needs of my other family. During my stay, Aretta, our daughter, came into the world on March 27, 1891. When Emma regained her strength and could care for the children, I journeyed back to Payson, resuming my farming endeavors.

Soon thereafter, I ventured into the world of breeding and raising thoroughbred horses. Additionally, I contributed my efforts to the D.R.&G. Railroad, transporting timber to Tintic for the construction of trestle work in Hommersville Canyon, and ferrying iron ore down to the railway.

In the early spring, I brought Emma from Teasdale and accompanied Ella from Payson, leading them to Salt Lake City for the April Conference and the momentous dedication of the Salt Lake Temple in April 1893. Subsequently, I escorted my wives back to their separate abodes. In June of that same year, Ella bore a son whom we named Harding, and on August 29, 1893, Samuel arrived into the world, born to Emma.

Samuel's Arrested and Charged:

However, the tide of persecution surged anew, prompting me to retreat into hiding. Thus, I returned to Teasdale, engaging in various endeavors such as working at the sawmill in the canyon and even tending to a flock of sheep, although the latter was unfamiliar territory for me. I did all in my power to evade detection. As autumn approached, I once again journeyed back to Payson, dedicating my time to the farm and hauling wood from the canyon to ensure a warm winter.

The subsequent summer was occupied by the cultivation of my land, and in the fall of 1894, I was taken aback when deputies surrounded my residence one morning. They presented me with an indictment and escorted me to Provo, where I was required to provide bonds for my appearance in court in Beaver the following November. Previously, my wife Emma had appeared before the grand jury that spring. My brothers John and James stood as my bondsmen.

It was during this period that Utah achieved statehood, with political tensions reaching their peak. I had made arrangements to travel to Beaver for the trial and, following the election, boarded a train to Milford, arriving there at nightfall. Fatigued and famished, I partook of sustenance and sought respite, but before retiring, I inquired of the innkeeper about the departure time of the stagecoach for Beaver in the morning.

To my dismay, I discovered that the stagecoach would depart immediately after the arrival of the train. I had missed it, and now found myself in a quandary, as I needed to reach Beaver by the next morning, the designated day for my court appearance. Upon inquiry, I learned that no one else was bound for Beaver. However, I inquired about a trail or a shortcut, and learned of a path that the soldiers had once traversed during their stay in Milford. The innkeeper informed me that Beaver lay approximately twenty-five miles away via this trail. I warned him not to be surprised if he heard me stirring early the next morning, for I had resolved to trek over the mountain.

The day proved scorching and arid, and upon reaching the Surrey, my progress became somewhat easier, until I embarked upon the long, parched stretch of land, bereft of anything but sagebrush. As nightfall descended, I reached Beaver, promptly securing a room at a hotel where I refreshed myself with a much-needed bath. Before partaking of supper, I encountered Judges Barch and McCarty, along with several distinguished attorneys, who engaged me in conversation. They were particularly curious about the progress of the elections, eager to learn of the outcome as I hailed from the north.

When Judge McCarty discovered my origin, he inquired about my name. After disclosing it, he appeared surprised, as my name had been called in court and my bonds had been declared forfeit due to my absence. I explained that I could clarify matters through Sam Thurman, the Prosecuting Attorney, who would be arriving the following day. The judge instructed me to be present in court the next morning, assuring me that he would explain the situation to the presiding judge and call my name.

Following a restful night's sleep and a hearty breakfast, I arrived at court punctually. As the session commenced, the court inquired if Mr. Francom was present. When I answered affirmatively, the clerk was directed to read the indictment, which accused me of adultery. Upon being asked for my plea, I declared myself "not guilty." I informed the judge of my readiness for trial, yet the prosecution was unprepared due to their inability to secure their primary witness. Consequently, the judge postponed my case until the May term, preserving my existing bonds.

Samuel's Polygamy Trial:

At that juncture, I sought out Attorney Thurman's office. Finding both attorneys in attendance, I requested their attention, explaining that my situation was somewhat intricate. I expressed my disapproval of the indecent nature of the indictment against me and reaffirmed my willingness to plead guilty to unlawful cohabitation if they would construct a more appropriate indictment.

They counseled me to appear before the Grand Jury in person and present my case. Judge McCarty accompanied me to the Grand Jury chamber. Upon entering the room, I recognized three familiar faces. Judge McCarty informed the Grand Jury that I was present to deliver a statement for their consideration.

The court was called to order. Judge McCarty commenced his inquiry, asking for my name, age, place of residence, and my relationship with Mrs. Emma Francom. He inquired about our marriage, the number and ages of our children, and whether I currently lived with her. I confessed that I hadn't seen her in eighteen months. When asked about her whereabouts, I revealed that we resided 200 miles apart. He dismissed me, promising to meet me in the morning. I spent the entire day in unease, pondering over what had transpired.

That night, I visited the men at their camp. Heber Wilson informed me that they found no indictment against me. I conversed with Judge McCarty, the Assistant Prosecutor, who revealed that they would have to detain me based on the old indictment. I returned to Mr. Wilson, sharing McCarty's words. I implored him to assist me by persuading the Grand Jury to reconsider when we entered the chamber, urging them to indict me for unlawful cohabitation. That evening, Judge McCarty conveyed the news that they had successfully obtained an indictment for unlawful cohabitation. He assured me that he would strive to expedite my case in the ongoing court term. Thus, I was compelled to wait for approximately ten days, spending a great deal of time listening to various cases.

At the end of this period, as the court proceedings drew to a close, my case was the final one on the docket. The Judge appeared eager to conclude the court session, having spent about fifteen days presiding over it. When McCarty informed him that the Francom case had been resolved, and I stood ready to enter a plea, the Judge responded curtly, stating that he had already dealt with it and that I was to appear in the May term. Mr. Thurman pleaded with the Judge to resolve the case while the defendant was present, to which the Judge reluctantly agreed. He instructed the clerk to read the indictment. "I plead guilty," I declared. Numerous thoughts raced through my mind, including the promise Apostle Young had made to me.

The Judge proceeded to interrogate me further. He inquired about the number of my children, their ages, the last time I had seen the woman, and if she had a home. He then elucidated my rights, stating that I was entitled to visit my children and have a companion accompany me. It was my responsibility to support and educate my children. He turned to Mr. Thurman and asked if he knew me and my character as a citizen. Mr. Thurman attested to my upstanding citizenship. Finally, the Judge addressed me, stating, "I must make an example of you. You are fined one dollar, plus court costs." As I went to pay the fine, the clerk advised me to keep the money, remarking that I was the luckiest man he had ever witnessed.

I journeyed alongside some of the men who served on the jury until Richfield, a distance of about forty miles. We reached Richfield late in the evening. From there, I took the stagecoach to Salina to catch a connecting train. The journey was pleasant but chilly. After boarding the train, it carried us northward through the canyon. The first stop was Thistle Junction, where I ordered a meal and barely had time to devour it before the train departed. I arrived in Springville around four p.m. and waited for approximately two hours for a train to transport me to Payson. When I arrived home, everyone was taken aback, as some had doubted I would regain my freedom.

After my prolonged absence, I had a great deal of farm work to attend to—digging potatoes, plowing for the upcoming season, hauling firewood for the winter, and so forth. In December, I returned to Teasdale and sold my property there. I relocated Emma and the family back to Payson, where they could receive better care and the children could benefit from improved educational opportunities.

My brother Jim accompanied me to assist in the move. In selling my Teasdale property, I had to accept a herd of cattle as payment. On April 1, 1885, we embarked on our journey from Teasdale with all our household possessions and the cattle, bound for Payson. Progress was slow, and we camped at Loa on the first night. The second night, we pitched camp on the divide between Grass Valley and Rabbit Valley. The snow, about four feet deep, had begun to melt, making travel arduous. We hired a man to transport a load of hay for our cattle, but it only lasted for three days. On the third night, we camped in Grass Valley.

From that point forward, we had to graze the cattle as we progressed. The weather became somewhat warmer, as we were now traversing the Sevier River Valley.

The fourth night, we set up camp on the western side of Salina, by the Sevier River. At this juncture, my brother Jim, along with the family and one of our teams, proceeded ahead. This left me and the boys to bring in the cattle.

The following night, we camped at Fayette. The cattle were growing weary, and we had to leave some behind. Our next stop was Levan, where my brother Joseph resided. After spending the night with him, we departed Levan and arrived in Payson the following morning.

I busied myself with settling Emma into her new home and procuring seed for the cattle. We had to purchase some furniture, including a new stove.

Around early May, we dedicated our efforts to branding the cattle before releasing them to roam the canyons. In those days, the range was open to all cattle. Alongside my farming responsibilities, I was occupied throughout the summer. I had an opportunity to sell some of the cattle, so one July morning, I set out early to gather them. I discovered a group of my cattle on a steep slope of the Lofer Mountains. As we descended, the slope grew so treacherous that my horse began to slip. I managed to dismount just in time as the horse tumbled over a cliff. I found her lifeless at the bottom. I removed the saddle and concealed it amidst the brush until I could retrieve it later. Consequently, I postponed the cattle roundup until the autumn season.

In the fall of 1895, I relocated Emma to another residence that was closer and more convenient for the children's schooling. I kept busy hauling wood for the two families and gathering my remaining stock. As autumn arrived, I sold the majority of my cattle— some for beef and others to Jesse Niles, a stockman. It was a relief to be relieved of the responsibility of such a sizable herd.

In December 1895, my wife Emma blessed me with another daughter, whom I named Ruth.

The following spring, I purchased a ranch from Hyrum Siler in Clinton, situated within Spanish Fork Canyon. In May 1896, I moved Emma and her family to this ranch. I also relocated the remaining stock that I had not sold, as it was closer to the range. We cultivated the farmland, sowing wheat and oats, and with the help of my sons, we reaped a bountiful harvest.

We stacked around 100 tons of hay, which I baled and sold at Thistle Junction. Additionally, we enjoyed a fruitful potato harvest, and I even experimented with growing watermelons. We made improvements to the house, constructing four additional rooms, a pantry, and closets, transforming it into a delightful six-room abode.

The bulk of my days were consumed with tending to two farms, but I also dedicated a considerable amount of time as Counselor to the esteemed Heber Johnson, Presiding Elder of Clinton. Our humble abode was always a welcoming haven for members of the Church who visited, as well as for political dignitaries and avid anglers from Salt Lake City and beyond.

During this period, I received the honorable ordination of High Priest and invested a great portion of my hours in Church endeavors.

It was in Clinton that Emma blessed me with my eighteenth and final child on December 19, 1897—a son whom we christened Stanley.

In 1902, my son George, then twenty-two years of age, received a sacred calling to embark on a mission to the Southeastern states. He was the first among my kin to heed such a divine summons.

Come the spring of 1902, I exchanged my farm and dwelling in Clinton with John Spencer for a dry farm and his homestead in Payson. We made our way to Payson in April of that year. Managing both farms kept us perpetually occupied. Horses grew scarce, prompting me to delve into the enterprise of breeding fine Percheron horses.

In 1903, I erected a new four-room dwelling on the property I had acquired from Spencer. We fashioned the abode from adobe bricks, toiling by hand in their creation. The subsequent spring of 1904 saw George's return from his mission. Soon thereafter, my son William was summoned to embark on a missionary journey to the Southern States, where he would spend over two years in service.

Around this juncture, I received a calling as a home missionary for the state of Utah and fulfilled my duties for a number of years. In 1914, I was called to undertake a mission to California, where I spent six months traversing the environs of Los Angeles and Orange County. Following my release, I journeyed to Arizona to visit my daughter, Estella Huber, who had established her residence there.

After departing from my daughter's abode in Arizona, I ventured to San Francisco to attend the World's Fair in 1915, spending several weeks in that vibrant city before returning to Salt Lake City. Upon my arrival in Salt Lake, a telegram informed me of the passing of my eldest brother, William, who had reached the age of sixty-five. He resided in Glenns Ferry, Idaho, at the time. I attended his funeral and lingered there for several days. Upon leaving Glenns Ferry, I made my way back to Payson, where I continued my labors as a home missionary, alongside other ecclesiastical duties.

Around this juncture, the Government commenced the construction of the Strawberry Project, and my dry farm fell under its irrigation system. As most of my children had entered the bonds of matrimony, I partitioned that portion of my farm among five of my sons: David, William, George, Elias, and Joseph. These were tumultuous times, as the United States found itself embroiled in war. Nonetheless, since all my sons were wedded, Samuel remained the sole individual to be called, and after valiantly serving two years across the seas, he safely returned home to us. As old age began to cast its shadow upon me, I resolved to sell my other farms, as land prices were particularly favorable at that juncture.

Upon advertising the sale of my farm, numerous inquiries regarding the price swiftly poured in. Concurrently, I made the decision to part with my farming equipment, cattle, horses—essentially everything save for our household furniture. Soon enough, a buyer materialized, and we reached a mutually agreeable price. After a few days, the transaction was finalized, the down payment handed to me, the necessary paperwork executed and signed. A moving date was set. On September 20, 1918, we bid farewell to our previous abode. For the time being, we took up residence in our son George's dwelling, as he had two rooms available for our use. We dwelt there until we discovered a suitable home. On February 5, 1919, we relocated to our current abode at 149 North First East Street in Payson.

Once we left the farm, I pondered whether I should undertake some efforts for the benefit of my deceased relatives. Fueled by this impetus, I journeyed to Salt Lake City and sought guidance at the Church Genealogy Library on how to embark upon this sacred task. During my visit, I acquainted myself with Mrs. Edith Barrett, who was diligently researching the Harding lineage—my maternal heritage—and also delving into the Francom side to some extent.

I engaged her services to assist me in uncovering genealogical information pertaining to the Francom ancestry, as I was primarily interested in my paternal lineage at that time.

I devoted numerous days to temple work, diligently fulfilling the sacred ordinances on behalf of our departed kin. Furthermore, I ensured that my father's siblings and brothers were sealed to their parents, as none of my brothers had taken up that noble cause, and as many of them had already passed away, it fell upon my shoulders to carry out this significant duty. Whenever the opportunity presented itself, I would journey to the temple and dedicate several days to this meaningful labor.

I have perpetually subscribed to the Desert News and maintained an unbroken readership of all Church magazines. Throughout this period, I remained an active home missionary and a devoted ward teacher.

During the winters of 1927 and 1928, Emma and I sojourned in Los Angeles for several months, dwelling alongside our sons Samuel and Stanley. I fondly recall the numerous excursions I embarked upon with my boys in and around the city, and the delight I experienced while exploring various places of interest with them.

One particular journey with Stanley stands out in my memory. We embarked on an expedition to San Bernardino, subsequently making our way to Arrowhead Lake. I had often heard tales of the renowned Arrowhead Trail and vividly recollected the accounts I had read and heard about the historic march of the Mormon Battalion—a valiant trek that covered half the continent, commencing from the prairies of Iowa in 1847 and 1848, culminating in a place now known as San Diego.

I recall Stanley acquainting me with the Arrowhead nestled amidst the mountains. We ventured up that canyon to discover a camp where men toiled, constructing roads. I encountered some locals who had dwelled in that vicinity for an extended duration. They regaled me with tales of the pioneering Mormon settlers and showcased a dilapidated wooden railroad used to slide timber down the steep slopes. It showcased the prudence and ingenuity of those early settlers. Our journey pressed on toward the mountaintop where they felled and fashioned lumber. A wagon they once employed still lingered there. The stumps of the trees bore the scorched marks of ropes utilized to guide the wagons down the timber slides.

From that vantage point, we beheld a splendid vista of Arrowhead Lake, ensconced within the profound abyss of the Sierra Nevada range. Eventually, the Battalion men were summoned back to Utah when Johnston's Army invaded the Mormon settlement. Consequently, they relinquished the city they had erected, which later found new inhabitants.

Emma and I returned to Payson in the spring of 1928, but in the subsequent winter of 1928 and 1929, we journeyed back to Los Angeles. It was during this sojourn that we commemorated our Golden Wedding anniversary with a jubilant gathering at my son Sam's abode. A total of twenty-six individuals attended, including Emma and me. Three sons, Elias, Sam, and Stanley; six grandchildren, Elias' six; three great-grandchildren; two nieces; two grand-nephews; and eight others related through marriage. Soon after, we made our way back to Payson.

In the year 1932, while engaged in Temple work in Salt Lake, illness befell me. The gravity of the situation necessitated calling a physician. At that time, I resided with my daughter Arreta, Mrs. John Smith. She suggested summoning Dr. Root, who, upon arrival, concluded that a prostate gland operation was imperative. I was then in my eightieth year, and the doctor harbored doubts about my ability to withstand such a serious procedure. Subsequently, I was admitted to the Holy Cross Hospital, where I received specialized care from a dedicated nurse. The kind Sister in charge ensured that all my needs were attended to. The Holy Cross Hospital exhibited a benevolent disposition towards the Mormon Elders who came to administer to their own people. The Church had specifically selected a group of Elders to minister to the sick if desired.

Despite the attentive care, my strength continued to wane. Although an abundance of food was provided, it failed to tempt my taste buds. After approximately sixteen days, my wife, daughter, and doctor conferred. The doctor proclaimed that I must eat, prompting Aretta to propose taking me to her home. When the doctor inquired if she comprehended the magnitude of the responsibility she was undertaking, she fearlessly replied, "I don't mind that aspect; just let us bring him home."

After reevaluating my condition, the doctor contacted Aretta, granting permission to retrieve me. The nurse attended to my wound as usual, while the elderly Sister inquired if I wished to rise from bed. Expressing my desire to do so, she retrieved my garments. It was at that moment that Mother and Aretta entered, declaring, "We are taking you home." A friendly rivalry ensued between the elderly Sister and the nurse, each vying to transport me to the waiting car. Ultimately, the elderly Sister emerged victorious.

I distinctly recall the beauty of that morning. Blooming flowers, lush foliage adorning the trees—it all seemed exquisitely beautiful. Aretta's home resembled a little paradise after the tribulations I had endured. I promptly retired to bed, while my loved ones diligently tended to my cleanliness and comfort. My appetite gradually improved, and each passing day witnessed a resurgence of strength. Within two weeks, I managed to traverse short distances on foot. Then, after another fortnight, they escorted me back to Payson. The return to my cherished home filled me with immense joy.

Approximately a year and a half later, I underwent another operation for hemorrhoids. This experience reinforced the wisdom of promptly addressing such matters, as both operations proved beneficial to my overall well-being.

On November 17, 1935, my beloved wife Ella was called Home, having lived to the age of 84. Ella was a virtuous and devoted wife, a kind and loving mother who blessed us with a fine brood of boys and girls. She departed this earthly realm in full fellowship, bearing the hope of a glorious resurrection.

In the verdant bloom of early Spring, in the year 1936, Aretta and her goodly spouse, John Smith, embarked on a wondrous journey to the distant lands of California. With swift wheels of steel, we traversed the expanse, passing through the glimmering domain of Las Vegas, Nevada, and ascending to Boulder City, where the mighty Boulder Dam stood in resolute grandeur. In my eighty-fourth year, my heart brimmed with anticipation, for the prospect of witnessing this marvel stirred within me an unruly delight. As we drew near the dam, I beheld with rapturous awe the deep gorge brimming with fortifying concrete, a bulwark against the torrential force of waters. With measured steps, I tread-ed the Dam's apex, journeying to the Arizona side, and in that very moment, my mind cast back to the stark contrast of 1888—a time when I crossed the tempestuous Colorado, beset by peril and trepidation. Contemplating the achievements of humankind, I marveled at the audacious feat of constructing this Mighty Dam, a means to subjugate that most treacherous river of Arizona.

Such a sight spurred within me a profound appreciation for the sagacity of man, far surpassing any prior reckonings. It awakened my understanding that the Divine had, indeed, bestowed His Spirit upon all mortals, facilitating the realization of His majestic designs upon this earthly realm.

Throughout my sojourn, I have steadfastly upheld my fidelity to Church and Government, striving to serve as a beacon of virtuous living for my kin. My households have harmoniously toiled alongside me, for both my wedded consorts and offspring have diligently heeded my guidance and acknowledged me as their venerable patriarch. This reflection fills my heart with a joyful pride as I survey the abundant assembly of my children, grandchildren, and a remarkable brood of fifty-three great-grandchildren. I sense that I have valiantly waged a righteous battle, remaining steadfast in my faith. And when my appointed hour arrives, at the culmination of my long and storied existence, I shall willingly surrender this mortal coil, entrusting my destiny to the merciful Hands of God.

The End.

A romanticized Story about my Great GrandFather Francom by Martin Francom

The Wisdom from O' Grandpa Francom

In 1910 at the small town of Glenns Ferry, Id, there lived a man, O' Grandpa Francom, William Henry Francom, a blacksmith by trade. He was a wise old soul, with a long white beard that flowed down to his chest and eyes that sparkled with the wisdom of a thousand years. His grandchildren adored him and often gathered around him, eager to listen to his tales and pearls of wisdom.

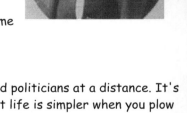

O' Grandpa Francom had a unique way of sharing his wisdom. Instead of delivering long lectures or preaching, he preferred to weave his words into stories, using humor and wit to make his lessons memorable. On warm summer evenings, as the sun dipped below the horizon, he would sit on his creaky wooden porch swing, the grandchildren nestled at his feet, and impart his timeless wisdom.

"Children," he would say with a twinkle in his eye, "I've learned a few things in my long years, and I reckon it's time I shared some of that knowledge with you. Pay close attention now, and remember these tidbits well."

"First and foremost," he began, "keep skunks, bankers, and politicians at a distance. It's a lesson that'll serve you well in life. Next, remember that life is simpler when you plow around the stump. Don't waste your time fretting over obstacles; find a way to work around them."

"Now, here's a fun fact for you," Grandpa Francom continued, chuckling. "A bumble bee is considerably faster than a John Deere tractor. It's a reminder that sometimes, small things can surprise you with their speed and power."

"Children, listen carefully," he cautioned. "Words that soak into your ears are whispered, not yelled. Pay attention to the quiet voices that offer wisdom and guidance. The best sermons are lived, not preached. Let your actions speak louder than your words."

"If you don't take the time to do it right," Grandpa Francom said, "you'll find the time to do it twice. Don't rush through life; do things properly the first time. And remember, don't corner something that is meaner than you. It's a surefire way to end up with a bruised ego."

"And please, oh please," he warned, wagging a finger, "don't pick a fight with an old man. If he's too old to fight, he'll just shoot you. Respect your elders and learn from their wisdom. It don't take a very big person to carry a grudge, but it weighs heavy on the heart. Learn to let go."

"You cannot unsay a cruel word," Grandpa Francom said, his voice filled with empathy. "Think before you speak, for words have the power to heal or hurt. Every path has a few puddles. Life is full of challenges, but it's how you navigate them that truly matters."

"When you wallow with pigs, expect to get dirty," he chuckled, emphasizing the importance of choosing your company wisely. "Don't be banging your shin on a stool that's not in the way. Avoid unnecessary troubles and focus on what truly matters."

"Borrowing trouble from the future doesn't deplete the supply," he grinned knowingly. "Most of the stuff people worry about ain't never gonna happen anyway. Don't waste your energy on needless worry."

"Don't judge folks by their relatives," Grandpa Francom advised. "Each person is unique, so judge them by their character and actions. And remember to listen and watch. Silence is sometimes the best answer. Not every question requires a response."

"Don't interfere with somethin' that ain't botherin' you none," he said with a sly smile. "Sometimes, it's best to let things be and focus on your own path. Timing has a lot to do with the outcome of a rain dance. Patience and proper timing can make all the difference."

Beware there are charlatans. No doubt in your life you will meet some.

They can weave a story so cleverly that you can become bamboozled. And if you are bamboozled long enough people tend to the reject out of hand any evidence of the bamboozle. It's simply too painful to acknowledge, even to yourself. So, keep a healthy skeptical mind. Watch out for politicians and preachers.

"If you find yourself in a hole, the first thing to do is stop diggin'," he said, his voice firm. "Acknowledge your mistakes and change your course. Sometimes you get, and sometimes you get got. Life isn't always fair, but how you react to it defines your character." "You may not be able to re-write your story to this point, but you can change the ending."

"The biggest troublemaker you'll ever have to deal with watches you from the mirror every mornin'," Grandpa Francom said, pointing at his reflection. "Take responsibility for your actions, and be the best version of yourself."

"Always drink upstream from the herd," he advised with a wink. "Learn to think independently and make your own choices. Good judgment comes from experience, and most of that comes from bad judgment.

Now, there are three types of people in this O'world: Dumb people, Smart people and Wise people. A smart person learns from his/her mistakes, a wise person learns from the mistakes of others and the dumb person continues to make the same mistake time after time. Don't be the dumb person, be wise. It will save you a world of grief."

"Lettin' the cat outta the bag is a whole lot easier than puttin' it back in," he chuckled. "Be cautious with the secrets you share; once they're out, you can't take them back."

"If you get to thinkin' you're a person of some influence, try orderin' somebody else's dog around," Grandpa Francom chuckled, reminding the children of the importance of humility and respect for others.

"Live a good, honorable life," he said, his voice filled with warmth. "Then when you get older and think back, you'll enjoy it a second time. Live simply, love generously, care deeply, speak kindly. Leave the rest to God."

"Most times, it just gets down to common sense," Grandpa Francom concluded, his eyes twinkling with wisdom. "Remember these tidbits, my darlings, and they'll guide you through life's twists and turns. And always remember, your old Grandpa loves you, each and every one of you."

And as the sun set, casting a warm glow over the porch, the children hugged Old Grandpa Francom tightly, feeling blessed to have such a wise and loving presence in their lives. They carried his wisdom in their hearts, knowing that his words would guide them on their journey through life.

####################

A Romanticized Story of The Francombe/Francom Crest

In the midst of the medieval period, in the year of our Lord 1060, there existed a quaint village nestled in the heart of Huntingdonshire, England. This village was known as FrankShire, and it was home to a nobleman by the name of William Samuel Francombe. As the Lord of the Manor, he ruled over his lands with a fair and just hand.

Now, in those days, when one wished to display their noble lineage and herald their family name, they adorned themselves with a coat of arms, a symbol of honor and identity. The creation of such a crest was a task not to be taken lightly, as it required careful consideration and a touch of artistic flair.

William Samuel Francombe, being a man of great ambition, sought to fashion a coat of arms that would not only reflect his lineage but also embody the spirit of his people. He wished for a crest that would represent the ideals of freedom and strength and most importantly wisdom, traits that he held dear in his heart.

With this in mind, Lord Francombe set about consulting the heralds and artisans of the land, seeking their expertise in crafting his family crest. Together, they delved into the depths of history, drawing inspiration from the ancient Anglo-Saxon roots of the Francombe name.

The Anglo-Saxon meaning of "Francombe" was "Free Man," a fitting moniker that resonated deeply with Lord Francom. He envisioned a crest that would encapsulate the very essence of this name, paying homage to the ideals of liberty and independence.

And so, after much contemplation and artistic deliberation, a magnificent design began to take shape. The crest would bear six ravens, those wise and cunning birds of the land, perched upon a flag adorned with two stripes one of yellow and one of purple. The ravens held significance beyond their mere avian form. Legends whispered of the birds' wisdom and foresight, their uncanny ability to navigate the intricacies of the world. To the Francombes, the ravens symbolized their indomitable spirit, their keen intellect, and their unwavering loyalty to kin and country. They served as guardians, watchful and observant, their keen eyes ever vigilant.

The Crest itself, with its vibrant yellow and regal purple stripes, represented the balance between freedom and nobility. Yellow, the color of the sun, stood for the warmth of liberty, represented hope, enlightenment, and prosperity while purple, associated with royalty, signified the dignity and honor inherent in the Francom lineage.

As the crest took its final form, Lord Francom marveled at the sight before him. It was a testament to the spirit of his family, a symbol that would be passed down through generations, forever etched in the annals of their noble history.

Word of the Francombe crest spread like wildfire throughout the land, capturing the imagination of all who heard of its creation. It became a symbol of inspiration and aspiration, a beacon of hope for the common folk who longed for freedom and sought to rise above the constraints of their station.

And so, in the year 1060, the Francombe Crest was born, a beacon of hope and an emblem of honor in a world where the echoes of battle still rang through the land. It served as a reminder that even in the face of adversity, the spirit of freedom would endure, carried forth by the blood and valor of the Francombes, the noble descendants of those who had once called these lands their own. After the Battle of Hastings in 1066 the Francombe name gradually lost it's medieval spelling and simply became Francom. The crest of the Francombe/Francom family came to be, a cherished emblem that not only honored their lineage but also stood as a reminder of the indomitable spirit of the English people. And though the Saxon influence waned after the Battle of Hastings, the legacy of the Francombe/Francom crest endured, forever etched in the tapestry of history.

#####################
Honoring the Sacrifices of Our Pioneers
In the 1860s, my kinfolk set out West,
Chasin' dreams, puttin' freedom to the test.
They left it all behind, seekin' a new start,
In Utah's territories, with a pioneer's heart.

With a twinkle in their eye and a spirit bold,
They aimed to build a ladder to the stars, I'm told.
Success or failure, they'd do it their own way,
Endurin' persecution, celebratin' come what may.

No city slickers, no cowards were they,
They faced the wild frontiers, day by day.
With grit and gumption, they forged their path,
Leavin' behind a legacy that would last.

They built America with their own two hands,
Lettin' freedom and free speech take their stand.
Strivin' for happiness, they never backed down,
Their descendants now reap the seeds they sowed 'round.

So let's raise a toast to these pioneers,
Those rugged souls who conquered their fears.
Their frontier wit, it still echoes loud and clear,
On this Fourth of July, let's give 'em a cheer.

With a nod and a wink, we honor their name,
Keepin' their spirit alive, burnin' like flame.

We're the product of their brave frontier roam,
So let's celebrate the freedom they called home.

With fireworks cracklin' and laughter in the air,
We gather 'round, grateful for what they did share.
On this day, let's tip our hats to the past,
And raise a glass to freedom that will forever last.

###################

Editors notes: Martin E. Francom with the help of GPT CHAT rewrote Samuel story in the folk style and added some information from Samuel older brother William Henry Francom which entries are marked by an editors note within the narrative.

Original Samuel's Story scanned and retyped by James P. Francom on 1 Dec 1996

This short autobiography came through Shawna Francom. Shawna got it from the Dean Francom Family in Payson Utah. The original manuscript was prepared by an "unknown (to me) relative" of Samuel Francom, living in Payson Utah. This document is provided "as is" to facilitate genealogical research of other members of the Francom family, and for it's human interest content. No attempt has been made to validate or correlate statements made by William or Samuel Francom with any other historical events. Many of the original documents can be found on the FamilySearch.com website.